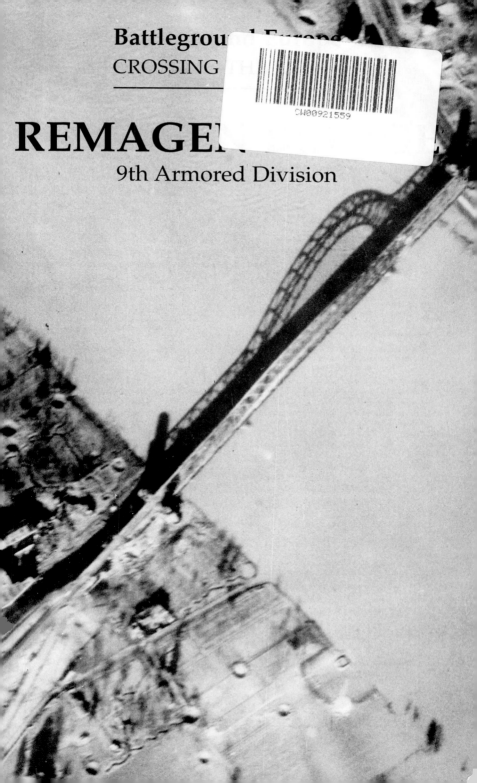

Battleground Europe
CROSSING

REMAGEN
9th Armored Division

Battleground Europe
CROSSING THE RHINE

REMAGEN BRIDGE
9th Armored Division

Andrew Rawson

LEO COOPER

Other books in the series by Andrew Rawson
Loos – Hill 70
Loos – Hohenzollern
Walcheren
Cherbourg

Published by
LEO COOPER
an imprint of
Pen & Sword Books Limited
47 Church Street, Barnsley, South Yorkshire S70 2AS
Copyright © Andrew Rawson 2004

ISBN 1 84415 036 4

A CIP catalogue of this book is available
from the British Library

Printed by CPI UK

*For up-to-date information on other titles produced under the Leo Cooper
imprint, please telephone or write to:*
Pen & Sword Books Ltd, FREEPOST, 47 Church Street
Barnsley, South Yorkshire S70 2AS
Telephone 01226 734222

CONTENTS

ACKNOWLEDGEMENTS

The capture of the Ludendorff Bridge at Remagen in March 1945 was one of those unplanned events in history, the consequences of which far outweigh the effort expended. Casualties were a fraction of other important engagements, and the number of men involved in the initial crossing only amounted to a few dozen. Yet the news that an intact bridge over the Rhine had been captured rocked the Western World. In America the event was considered to be so important that the meeting in progress at the US Senate was halted to announce the news. Many books have been written about the crossing of the bridge, and in 1969 Wolper Pictures Limited produced an action packed film based on the events at Remagen. This book is not about Hollywood, it is an attempt to describe the events leading up to the capture of the bridge and the fierce fighting that followed on the east bank of the Rhine, an aspect that has been overlooked in previous accounts. Crossing the bridge at Remagen was only the start of the battle and many GIs memories of Rhineland focus on the battle for the Westerwald. Hopefully, the balance is right.

A number of people have helped me write this book, and my research would have been incomplete without their assistance. All the staff at the US National Archives in Washington DC, made me feel extremely welcome and helped to make my visit to the USA both fruitful and memorable. There are, however, a handful of people who took me under their wing and deserve a special mention. In particular I would like to thank David Giodarno, who initially gave me a guided tour through the printed documents archives and continued to keep an eye on my progress, giving useful tips as the days passed; his assistance was invaluable. Beth Lipford's ongoing guidance as I worked through the indexing system to order documents meant that I received the material I wanted in good time. Meanwhile, Tom McAnear worked hard to locate and copy the maps I required in the cartography room. Holly Reed in the photographic department also made sure that I obtained the photographs I needed. As my departure date drew near, everyone worked hard to make sure that I collected the material I required; customer service is certainly uppermost in the minds of the staff at the NARA.

Kurt Kleemann, curator of the Brücke von Remagen (Bridge at Remagen) museum has been particularly helpful. During our long meeting at his office, I was able to discuss many of the myths that surround the capture of the bridge. A second opinion from someone who has studied the events at Remagen for years proved invaluable, dispelling a number of doubts I had concerning the events on 7 March 1945. I would also like to thank Herr Kleemann for giving me permission to use a number of photographs from the museum's collection, depicting German subjects. They have helped to give the book the balance I wanted.

Following the capture of the bridge the Germans attempted to bring it down by various means – here an artillery shell explodes in the Rhine.

Although I never knew them and probably never shall, I will always have a high regard for the men who kept the Army records in March 1945. Their unit diaries, signal records, after-action reports and interviews have formed the basis for my research. The records were put together under difficult circumstances and one particular report, the signal records for the 14th Tank Battalion, brought it home to me that these reports were taken in real time. Line after line of messages fill the pages, each one timed and referenced; an invaluable aid to the historian wishing to track the events as they unfold. Yet the thing that struck me was that the handwriting was shaky; this man was on the move as he made his notes, sat at the side of his officer as their Jeep drives towards Remagen. Only on this day he will record the capture of a bridge that will be front page news across the world and later be described by Eisenhower as *'worth its weight in gold'*. Without records like these it would have been impossible to write this book.

As my own son Alex approaches his teenage years and watches world events unfold on the television, I am reminded that young men are still going to war, leaving their families and loved ones behind. They have the same hopes and fears as those soldiers at Remagen in March 1945; let us never forget that.

CHAPTER ONE

REMAGEN – A BRIEF HISTORY

Remagen's Background

The Romans established the original settlement on the west bank of the Rhine. Drusus, commander of the Army of the Rhine, built over fifty forts along the river between 16BC and 12BC to protect the Empire from marauding tribes. One fort was Ricomagus, a crossing point situated where the river sweeps gracefully past the foot of Erpeler Ley, a huge basalt outcrop. The settlement dealt with trade heading into and out of Gaul for over five hundred years, before the disintegration of the Roman Empire in the face of the Huns, forced an evacuation from the Rhineland.

The Rhine witnessed turbulent times over the centuries that followed and future settlers on the banks of the river faced invasion and occupation by a succession of warring tribes. Despite setbacks the town continued to thrive as a significant crossing over the Rhine. Although the end of the Dark Ages signified a new period of peace a new conflict, the Thirty Years War, marked the start of a series of raids on the town. Between 1631 and 1633 ninety per cent of the town was razed to the ground as Swedish Troops engaged Imperial and Spanish soldiers in a struggle for southwest Germany. At the turn of the Seventeenth Century large parts of Remagen were again destroyed as British and French Armies waged war during the Wars of the Spanish Succession. A century later Napoleon's soldiers exacted their revenge on the inhabitants of Remagen before they were driven back by Russian troops. Each time, the people of the town returned to the west bank of the Rhine to rebuild their homes.

By the turn of the twentieth century the town had developed into a fashionable resort, relying on its charming position to attract tourists to the area. Many flocked to Remagen to take advantage of the fantastic views along the river, or to use the town as a base for walking holidays in the Rhineland.

In 1914 Europe was once again plunged into turmoil as the Allies and Central Powers clashed at the start of the Great War. During the build up to the world conflict, German military planners had recognised the need for additional crossings over the Rhine. Although the river had acted as a defensive barrier in the past, it would restrict the volume of traffic required to transport troops from Central Germany into France and Belgium. Three bridges were planned to accommodate the rapidly expanding rail network connecting Germany's border regions, the Saar and the Eifel. Despite the advice given by the military, construction of a new rail link across the Rhine at Remagen was postponed indefinitely.

Although Germany's military plan for war, the Schlieffen Plan, was designed to knock France out within a matter of weeks, by mid-September 1914 a series of setbacks found the German Armies in full retreat. Following the Battle of the Marne and the so-called Race to the Sea that followed, Germany found itself on the defensive in the West. The Central Powers were fighting a two front war, requiring an efficient cross-country rail network to keep men and materials flowing to the front. Faced with this new strategic situation, General Erich von Ludendorff, the German Chief of Staff, resurrected part of the pre-war construction plan and sanctioned the building of two new river crossings; a road bridge in the city of Cologne and a rail bridge at the town of Remagen.

Design work began immediately on the Remagen project, a rail link connecting the Ruhr and the Ahr valley. A series of natural

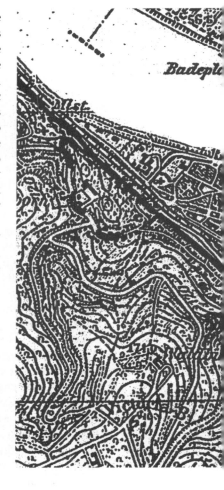

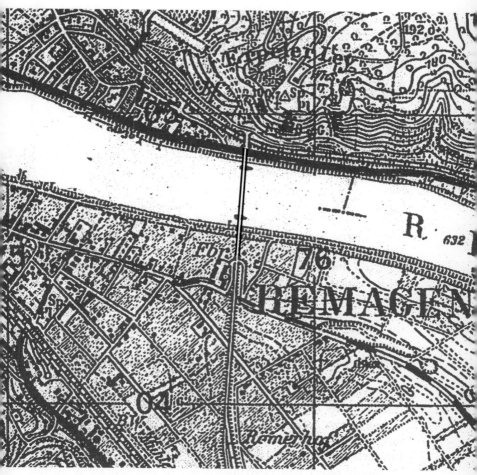

Remagen's position on the banks of the Rhine ensured continuing prosperity for its population.

obstacles would test the chosen architect, Karl Wiener, to his limits. The Rhine, a fast flowing river over three hundred and fifty metres wide, was only one of three problems faced by the engineers. Wiener proposed a symmetrical three span bridge, supported by two piers in the river. The deck had to be fifteen metres above water level to give adequate clearance for passing river traffic. It meant that a railway viaduct had to be built on the west bank, to carry the railway across the river valley. The construction team on the east side of the river faced a completely different obstacle. Erpeler Ley, the steep rocky outcrop, rose one hundred and seventy five metres above the river. A short tunnel had to be driven through the basalt, so that the rail link could connect with the direct line from Bonn to Frankfurt.

Construction work commenced in 1916 and for two years the people of Remagen looked on as the structure began to grow. The engineering teams progressed as quickly as possible and with limitless funds of money available, the project was finished on time. The bridge carried twin rail tracks across the Rhine and pedestrian walkways flanked the tracks. It meant that the inhabitants of Remagen and Erpel would be able to cross the river without having to rely on the ferry.

Although the bridge had been designed primarily for military traffic, the local residents were please to note that it was sympathetic to the eye. The central span, measuring over one hundred and seventy metres wide, took the form of a bowstring arch, two smaller spans, each one over one hundred metres wide, connected the piers to the riverbanks. Twin turreted towers stood on each bank, guarding the approaches to the bridge, and although they looked like architectural features to the casual observer, they were designed as guard towers. Each tower was capable of housing dozens of men and gun embrasures in the turret walls would make sure that no one could capture the bridge without a fight. A battalion of men could live in the towers and, if necessary, fight from any of the three storeys. Lookout platforms at the top of each tower made sure that the garrison could see an enemy approaching from miles away. Tunnels beneath the tracks, connecting each pair of towers, completed the formidable bastions.

The architect had been instructed to incorporate a further defensive feature in his design, in case there was a danger that the bridge could fall into enemy hands. The two bridge piers were built as hollow shells, complete with demolition chambers. Several tonnes of explosives could be installed at the base of the piers in case it came under attack. Electrical circuits, protected by steel tubing, had been included so engineers would be able to detonate the bridge from the safety of the rail tunnel beneath the Erpeler Ley.

The rail connection was finally completed in 1918 at the same time as a new road bridge in Cologne, forty kilometres downstream. A dual dedication ceremony followed and the two

American troops cross the Ludendorff Bridge in December 1918.
Friedensmuseum

new crossings were named in honour of the military partnership responsible for leading the German Army; the Hindenburg Bridge at Cologne and the Ludendorff Bridge at Remagen. Although rail traffic was soon speeding across the bridge, it had no effect on the outcome of the war and a few months later, on 11 November 1918, the Armistice was declared. Before long the first troops of the American Expeditionary Force crossed the bridge on their way into the heart of Germany.

Thousands more Allied troops had crossed before the Rhineland was handed over to French control in 1919. The French authorities were concerned that saboteurs might try to destroy the rail bridge and their engineers filled the demolition chambers, built as an integral part of the piers, with concrete.

General Ludendorff. The bridge at Remagen was named in his honour.

13

During the 1920s deep economic depression across Germany reduced the flow of trains across the bridge to a bare minimum. Businesses could rarely pay to transport their goods by rail and few people could afford to travel by train. For years the bridge stood virtually idle, reduced to little more than a footbridge connecting Remagen with the east bank of the Rhine.

As Germany's fortunes turned in the 1930s, rail traffic across the Ludendorff Bridge increased dramatically. Large numbers of troops were transported west during the reoccupation of the Rhine land in 1936, at the start of Germany's expansion across Europe. Rearmament of the Germany Army meant that the Ludendorff Bridge was, once again, being used for its original purpose.

In 1938, as the political situation with France deteriorated, German engineers took steps to prepare the bridge for an emergency demolition. The 'sabotage' carried out by their French counterparts in filling in the demolition chambers called for a new approach. It was impractical to remove the concrete from the chambers inside the piers so, instead, the engineers took steps to prepare the superstructure for demolition.

The engineers installed a series of zinc-lined containers on key structural members. If the need arose explosive charges could be placed in the protective boxes ready for detonation. The ignition wiring was laid in steel tubing to protect the cables from accidental damage and a system of circuit testers was installed so that regular checks could be carried out on the wiring. An additional manual system was installed as a back up to the main circuitry. Primer cords, that could be ignited by hand, were on standby in case the electrical system failed. Nothing had been left to chance. The guards billeted at the bridge could destroy the rail crossing with the minimum of preparation.

Sightseeing along the Rhine between the wars. Schleef/Friedensmuseum

As businesses flourished under the National Socialists there were concerns that a new autobahn, connecting Bonn and Koblenz, would ruin the charm of the town. The local population were pleased to see that the planners eventually routed the highway around the outskirts of Remagen. Dr Hans Kemming assumed the role of Burgomaster in 1932 and immediately took steps to improve facilities in the town for visiting tourists. His main project was a new riverside promenade to allow visitors to enjoy the views along the Rhine in safety.

However, while the 1930s brought prosperity to many, it was the start of a life of deprivation and fear for some inhabitants of the town. The rise of National Socialism and the wave of anti-Semitism that followed introduced a series of laws aimed at restricting the Jewish community. Businessmen were forced to hand over their properties for a fraction of their value or face deportation to one of the many labour camps springing up

The Bridge Security Company during the first winter of the war.
Stang/Friedensmuseum

across the country. The burning of Remagen's synagogue in November 1938 during *Kristallnacht*, a night of destruction and humiliation sanctioned by the National Socialists, signified the start of an exodus of the Jewish community.

Remagen during the war

Although the Rhine crossings received little attention during the early stages of the war, there was a need to maintain a military presence at the bridges. 2/12th River Security Company, led by *Feldwebel* Jakob Kleebach, manned Remagen Bridge from the outbreak of war, and spent their time monitoring traffic across the river. In the summer of 1943 the VI Military District, an organisation responsible for internal security, took steps to increase the number of troops based along the Rhine. The 3rd Battalion of the 12th Territorial Regiment was allocated the stretch of river between Bonn and Koblenz and Company 12, under the command of forty-eight year old *Hauptmann* Karl Friesenhahn, was given responsibility for the Ludendorff

Bridge. Friesenhahn, a veteran of the First World War, had been discharged from the Army after he had been wounded for the third time. He was recalled during the build up to the Second World War and given command of a non-combat unit.

The Allied landings in Normandy in June 1944 meant that there was a need for increased security along the Rhine. The 80th Infantry Replacement and Training Battalion was formed in Koblenz, and one of its companies was stationed at Remagen. The commander, forty-year old *Hauptmann* Willi Bratge, had served as an army training officer in the Reichswehr and had been recalled as a reservist as Germany prepared to invade Poland. He saw

Hauptmann **Karl Friesenhahn, bridge Commandant, and his wife.**

17

Hauptmann Willi Bratge

active service in Poland and France and after a brief period as a training officer, returned to the front line. Bratge was seriously wounded in Russia and on his recovery he was given a non-combat role.

The men under Captain Bratge were convalescing soldiers, and during their stay at Remagen many made daily visits to the local hospitals to have their dressings replaced. Although Bratge tried to take steps to build defensive works around the bridge, his work was frustrated by the lack of supplies and active men. Over the winter months Captain Bratge managed to build a series of outposts along the Victoriasberg heights west of the town. He also set up a guardroom in the *Waldberg Hotel* overlooking Remagen, so that his men could keep in contact with his headquarters at St Anne's Convent in the town. Following the Allied breakout from Normandy in August 1944 Remagen was suddenly thrust into the spotlight when United States Air Force planners were ordered to target the German rail network. The Ludendorff Bridge was an ideal target; if the bombers managed to destroy the bridge it would seriously restrict the flow of men and supplies across the Rhine.

Throughout September, the Ninth US Air Force carried out a series of daylight bombing raids on the rail crossings at Düsseldorff, Cologne, Remagen and Koblenz. The VI Military District responded by deploying engineering units to maintain and repair the bridges along the Rhine. Although it was difficult to hit a target as small as a bridge, hopes were raised on 19 October when US 36th Bombing Group reported that it had destroyed the Ludendorff Bridge. Reconnaissance photographs later showed the bridge had only suffered superficial damage and within two weeks the German 103rd Railway Engineer Company and a company of the 1st Technical Battalion had managed to reopen it for rail traffic.

Flak units were deployed on the heights to defend the bridge and although the majority possessed light 37mm and 20mm AA guns, the 1/535th Heavy Railway Detachment provided the backbone of the anti-aircraft defences. A company of artillerymen armed with smoke generators was also deployed around the bridge.

Although the bombers had little success in hitting the bridge itself, many bombs fell in and around the town. as a consequence the inhabitants of Remagen came to despise the structure. The majority of the men folk had already left to fight at the front, and women, children and elderly left behind had to adapt to a frightening daily routine. After spending the morning queuing for rationed food, many fled into the hills and woods to escape the afternoon bombing raids. Once the all clear had sounded the town once more came alive, as the population returned to clear up the rubble, hoping that their own home had survived. Despite the danger of living in what amounted to a target zone, some refused to leave the town. Over the course of the winter of 1944/45 over sixty inhabitants of Remagen lost their lives in the raids.

In November, the US Air Force changed tactics, targeting railway junctions and Sinzig rail junction, three miles south of Remagen, was attacked a number of times. Although there appeared to be no chance of permanently severing the rail link by bringing the bridge down, continued raids succeeded in severely disrupting the flow of traffic through the Ahr valley. Following the German offensive in the Ardennes during December, the Allied planners turned their attention to the Rhine crossings once more. The people of Remagen faced a bleak Christmas as the bombers renewed their efforts to destroy the bridge. Finally, during a raid on 29 December, several bombs caused extensive damage to the viaduct and although the superstructure was unharmed, engineers estimated that it would take several weeks to repair the damage.

Throughout the winter *Hauptmann* Bratge's men were recalled to the front line as soon as they were deemed fit for active service and although the 105th Convalescent Battalion

The temporary repairs to the damaged viaduct. US SC NARA/Friedensmuseum

sent replacements, by February 1945 the company strength had dwindled to a few dozen men. At the beginning of the month a new flak battery, the 3/900th Flak Training and Test Battery arrived at Erpel. First Lieutenant Karl Peters' battery was armed with experimental rocket launchers, known as *Föhngeräte* and as the batteries deployed on the slopes above the village, they raised considerable interest among the rest of the flak crews in the area.

The people of Remagen watched the increase of military traffic in the area and few doubted that, before long, their town would be in the battle zone. Meanwhile, the Allies were planning their new offensive and the problem uppermost in the their minds was, how to cross the Rhine.

CHAPTER TWO

THE ADVANCE TOWARDS GERMANY

Following the breakout from Normandy and the Battle for Falaise, the Allied Armies streamed east across France and for a few short weeks it seemed as though the German Army had been broken. Meanwhile, 9th Armored Division had left New York at the end of August 1944 bound for Scotland and, after a short acclimatisation period, moved to the south coast of England to receive new tanks and equipment.

There were high hopes for an early conclusion to the war as autumn approached, however, the Allied planners faced a new problem; the advancing columns were outstripping their supply lines. Although supplies were building up along the Normandy coast, the Red Ball Express, comprising endless lines of lorries been driven day and night, was struggling to cope with the demands of the front line troops. As winter approached the problem would increase as bad weather closed the temporary harbours for long periods. Allied attempts to capture one of the Channel Ports intact had been frustrated by German rearguards. On each occasion, German engineers managed to destroy the harbour facilities before they could be taken.

As summer came to an end, Eisenhower was forced to prioritise his plans in the face of rivalry between 21 Army Group's commander, Field Marshal Bernard Montgomery, and 12 Army Group's CO, General Omar Bradley. While Montgomery's troops raced across northern France heading for Belgium and Holland, the First US Army was driving across the southern part of Belgium and General George S Patton's Third Army was passing to the south of Luxembourg heading north east for the Rhine. All three commanders wanted to spearhead the way into Germany. However, the shortfall in supplies meant that Eisenhower could only support one offensive. Montgomery planned to drop three airborne divisions, capturing the bridges across the Maas and Neder Rein (the Dutch name for the Rhine) by surprise. An armoured column would then push into northern Germany, advancing north of the Ruhr. General Hodges, First US Army's commanding officer, wanted to force a crossing of the Rhine around Cologne and Bonn, in the hope of taking the Saar coalfields.

September saw the Allied advance slow to a crawl as the supply crisis deepened. Meanwhile, the German Armies had begun to regroup as *Feldmarschall* Model began to formulate plans to defend his homeland. Meanwhile, Eisenhower had decided to follow Montgomery's plan and on 17 September the skies over Holland were filled with planes and gliders as Operation MARKET GARDEN began. Almost at once the operation faltered and the 101st and 82nd American Airborne Divisions faced fierce counterattacks as they tried to maintain a corridor between Eindhoven and Nijmegen for the British armoured column. The anticipated rapid advance towards the Neder Rein never materialised and the 1st British Airborne Division found itself isolated and outnumbered at Arnhem, on the north bank of the river.

Major-General John W Leonard, commander of the 9th Armored Division.
National Archives 111-SC-200522

Within a few days the hopes for a rapid advance into northern Germany had been dashed, leaving Eisenhower to confront his supply problem. Although Antwerp had fallen into Allied hands at the beginning of August, it would take three months to clear German troops from the Schelde estuary and open the port for supplies.

After completing its training, Major-General Leonard's Division sailed to France during October and made its way east into Belgium. As his men adapted to life in the front line in a quiet sector facing the Siegfried Line west of Prüm, the battles for 'Bloody' Aachen and the Hürtgen Forest raged on, draining American resources.

Throughout the winter generals continued to put forward plans for an advance into Germany. Montgomery wanted to continue where Operation MARKET GARDEN had ended, while Bradley proposed a pincer movement, north and south of the Ruhr, intending to deprive Germany of its main industrial centre. This time Eisenhower chose to support Bradley, relegating Montgomery's Army Group to a subsidiary role. The First and Third US Armies would advance towards the Rhine, in the hope of establishing a bridgehead on the east bank. To release troops for the forthcoming attacks, other sectors of the line would be kept on the defensive; one such area was southern Belgium.

After a few weeks at the front the 9th Armored Division had withdrawn to Luxembourg to carry out more training. Their lull in the fighting was shattered on 17 December when the Germans launched their offensive in the Ardennes. The 9th Armored Division was immediately called upon to help contain the breakthrough. The two Combat Commands were committed to different sectors; one was sent to help defend Luxembourg City while the second headed to Bastogne to help the 101st Airborne Division defend the vital road junction. Germans posing as American soldiers had caused panic in the St Vith sector and Combat Command Battalion (CCB) entered the line as German troops advanced in the wake of the confusion caused. 27th Armored Infantry Battalion became embroiled in the fighting around Malmedy and a number of troops were cut off. They were later found murdered by *Kampfgruppe* Pieper just outside the town. The headquarters company also became separated from the rest of the battalion on the night of the 21st. The intelligence officer managed to slip through the German lines under cover of darkness and located the rest of his unit. With the information he provided the battalion was able to launch a the following day, rescuing the staff from capture.

The 9th Armored Division suffered heavy casualties in the confused fighting and on two occasions German communiqués announced that the division had been destroyed. As the survivors withdrew to reorganise on 23 December they christened themselves the 'Phantom Division'. The Germans would be hearing a lot about the 9th Armored Division in the coming months.

The start of 1945 brought new challenges as the First and Third American Armies drew close to the Siegfried Line. Yet again there were differences of opinion on how to enter Germany but Eisenhower decided to allow Montgomery to take the lead role, pushing south between the Maas and Rhine rivers. Meanwhile, Hodges First US Army would advance north towards Bonn in the hope of trapping thousands of German troops in a pincer movement behind the Siegfried Line.

9th Armored Division continued to train during the early weeks of 1945 but at the end of February the division returned to the front line, joining III Corps as it prepared to cross the Röer River.

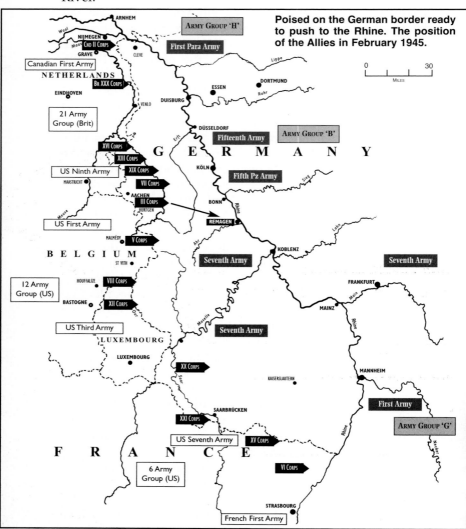

Poised on the German border ready to push to the Rhine. The position of the Allies in February 1945.

CHAPTER THREE

THE ADVANCE TO THE RHINE

First US Army's advance offensive began at the beginning of February in atrocious weather. As General Hodge's divisions moved forward at a snail's pace melting snow churned up the countryside, confining tanks and vehicles to muddy roads. As they drew close to the Röer German engineers sabotaged reservoirs, turning the river into a raging torrent.

In response to the American advance, a number of changes in the German command structure took place along the Rhine. In XII Corps area, the military district of Wiesbaden had only taken over control for the Remagen area at the beginning of February, when, on the 26th, it was warned that it would be handing over its responsibilities to the Field Army. Although the order was a tactical decision, an army needed control of its rear area to a

Thick mud severely restricted First Army's advance. National Archives 111-SC-202207

depth of approximately fifteen miles to control the flow of troops and supplies to the front line, it would raise potential problems. Rivalries between the *Feldheer* (Field Army) and the *Ersatzheer* (Replacement) Army often caused friction as control was handed over.

Two days later *Hauptmann's* Bratge and Friesenhahn were informed that they would, in future, report to *Leutnantgeneral* Botsch, the new commandant for the stretch of the Rhine between Bonn and Remagen. Fifth Panzer Army's take over from XII Army Corps was further complicated by a reorganisation of the front line. Gerd von Rundstedt wanted his Panzer Armies withdrawn from the line to form a mobile reserve and on the night of 28 February General von Zangen's Fifteenth Army entered the front line. LXVII Corps, under General Otto Hitzfeld, held the sector between Schmidtheim and Münstereifel, which ultimately held responsibility for the Remagen area. Although the corps looked impressive on paper, the two divisions under its command could only muster 1,500 men and about forty artillery pieces.

On 28 February Operation GRENADE began when landing craft carried the first wave of troops across the Röer. Cables strung across the river guided DUKWs and amphibious tanks through the fast flowing current and as the bridgehead expanded,

DUKWs were indispensable for ferrying troops across the Röer.
National Archives 111-SC-203737

Troops of the 9th Armored Division clear Euskirchen en route to the Rhine.
National Archives 111-SC-281971

engineers began to build bridges supported by pontoons and huge inflatables. It seemed to some as though it was a dress rehearsal for what lay ahead – the crossing of the Rhine.

9th Armored Division had just joined General John Millikin's III Corps and it made its way across the river in the wake of 78th Infantry Division. For the next few days CCB would act in a supporting role to the infantry as they advanced towards the Rhine.

Beyond Vetweiss Brigadier-General William M Hoge ordered his troops to split into three armoured columns and managed to establish a bridgehead across the Neffel River. The following day CCB encountering German rearguards and the centre column ran into strong anti-tank gun positions beyond Sievernich, losing four Sherman tanks. It was a

Major General Millikin.

sharp reminder that the Germans were far from beaten.

Although 1 March saw the advance slow to a crawl, CCB managed to reach Neiderberg on the 2nd and was fortunate enough to capture the bridge in the centre of the town. It gave Brigadier Hoge a chance to reorganise his men and during the early hours of 3 March, 27th Armored Infantry Battalion drove through the night to reach Lommersum. As Major Murray

Deevers men entered the town German engineers destroyed the bridge over the River Erft. Attempts to cross the river during daylight hours failed and it was only after two infantry companies made a crossing, under the cover of darkness, were the engineers able to start building a bridge.

In the meantime, CCB were sent south through Bodenheim and after a second night advance, managed to cross the Erft and take Wuscheid and Grossebullesheim without a shot being fired. At least it seemed as though the Germans were in full retreat and as 27th Armored Infantry Battalion made its way through Miel heading for Morenhoven and Flerzheim, 52nd Armored Infantry Battalion joined CCB ready for the final stage of the advance to the Rhine.

While the First US Army advanced towards Bonn, General von Botsch toured the Rhine to meet his subordinates. He discovered that *Hauptmann* Bratge had only thirty-six men under his command and, although there were *Hauptmann* Friesenhahn's engineers and the crews of AA guns in the vicinity, more men would be needed to defend the bridge. During his last visit to Remagen, on 5 March, von Botsch promised to send a battalion of men to assist Bratge.

As 6 March dawned, CCB was preparing to advance towards its next objective, Stadt Meckenheim, only eight miles from the Rhine. Meanwhile, in Remagen troops were filing over the Ludendorff Bridge to escape the American spearheads.

Keeping watch on the bridge.
Hoffmann/Friedensmuseum

CHAPTER FOUR

OVERNIGHT PREPARATIONS

Overnight in Stadt Meckenheim

Combat Command B (CCB) advanced through Esch on the afternoon of 6 March and as 27th Armored Infantry Battalion advanced towards Morenhoven, Brigadier-General William M Hoge ordered his second battalion, the 52nd, to move forward in support. Although Hoge expected a long drawn out battle for the town, his men could see white flags as they entered the town. Flerzheim had also been abandoned by fleeing German troops and although it seemed as though CCB was at long last making good progress, ahead lay Stadt Meckenheim, a potential bottleneck.

Brigadier-General William Hoge. National Archives 111-SC-200521

Tanks and halftracks line the streets waiting for the order to advance.
National Archives 111-SC-335254

27th Armored Infantry Battalion came under fire as it entered the town during the late afternoon and although the 52nd was close behind resistance quickly came to an end as the infantry and tanks worked their way through the streets. After Brigadier Hoge had set up his headquarters in the town he ordered the 52nd Armored Infantry Battalion to reorganise in Flerzheim overnight; the 27th would billet in Stadt Meckenheim along with the 14th Tank Battalion. Although the GIs were used to seeing bomb damaged towns, the devastation caused by the USAFs bombing raids on Meckenheim was extraordinary; many buildings had been destroyed, leaving the local population homeless. Huge mounds of rubble, in some places over two metres high, blocked many of the streets and the tanks crews and GIs were forced to stand by and watch as the engineers set to work clearing a road through. Although tanks equipped with bulldozers joined the clear up operation, it would still take many hours before vehicles could move along the high street.

Brigadier Hoge's original orders called for an advance northeast the following morning, towards Lannesdorf. Meanwhile, 9th Armored Division's second Combat Command

(CCA) would advance east towards Remagen and Sinzig. Taking note of the roads leading out of Meckenheim, Hoge decided to spilt his command into two task forces, each one comprising of a mix of tanks and infantry mounted in halftracks. The armoured columns were expected to meet little resistance and it was hoped that they would be able to make good progress, reaching the Rhine by midday. Armoured cars of the 89th Reconnaissance Squadron would scout the route ahead, looking for signs of enemy roadblocks.

Whenever a German rearguard was located, the column would prepare to engage the enemy. Usually the infantry would dismount, fanning out across the fields to outflank the position while the tanks and halftracks provided supporting fire. The tanks would also target suspected strong points or enemy armour. The tactics had worked well and in many cases poorly equipped rearguards surrendered after putting up a token defence.

Brigadier Hoge planned to send the 27th Armored Infantry Battalion, supported by Company A of the 14th Tank Battalion, in a north easterly direction, while the 52nd Armored Infantry Battalion, supported by Company A of the 14th Tank Battalion headed east through Adendorf. However, before his plan had been formalised, Major-General Leonard issued a new set of orders. CCB was to advance southeast towards Sinzig on the River Ahr.

At first the order caused confusion. Hoge was convinced that CCA was supposed to take the two towns but the new instruction meant that the two commands would be advancing at right angles, overlapping en route. After querying the order with his commanding officer, Hoge received detailed instructions at 03:30 am, clearing up the confusion. CCA's route had been shifted south and was expected to capture Bad Neuenahr. Meanwhile, CCB had two objectives. The main thrust would be southeast, with the intention of capturing the crossings over the River Ahr at Bodendorf and Sinzig. The Division would then be able to continue to push south along the Rhine towards Seventh Army. It was hoped that the pincer movement would trap thousands of Germans before they could escape across the river.

CCB's subsidiary objective was to clear the west bank of the Rhine around Remagen. Reconnaissance troops would cover the left flank of the advance, scouting the area west of Bad Goesburg. It was known that the Germans were destroying the bridges over the Rhine once their own troops had crossed. Orders issued by III Corps mentioned the Ludendorff Bridge at Remagen. Once the artillery was in range it was directed to use time, or pozit, fuses only. Thus exploding shells would cause casualties but leave the structure undamaged. No one expected to capture the bridge intact, yet, the possibility was briefly discussed at a higher level. During a telephone conversation, General Millikin remarked to Major-General Leonard, 'Do you see that little black strip of bridge at Remagen? If you happen to get that, your name will go down in glory'. In less than twenty-four hours that casual comment would take on a new meaning.

While the 27th and 52nd Armored Infantry Battalions spent a restful night waiting for new orders, 9th Armored Division's third armoured infantry battalion, the 60th, was on the move. Lieutenant-Colonel Collins had split his task force into three groups, each containing a rifle company and a tank platoon. The plan was to drive quickly through the night, in the hope of cutting off thousands of German troops heading for the Rhine

Tanks of the 9th Armored Division advance across country. National Archives 111-SC-203638

and Collins' had ordered his company commanders to keep moving, avoiding contact with the enemy if at all possible. The three groups would advance in column, swapping the lead when a company ran low on ammunition.

At dusk the 60th Armored Infantry Battalion set off, heading south through Altendorf and Gelsdorf and as they travelled through the night the GIs encountered hundreds of Germans heading for the Rhine. The appearance of the armoured column passing by shocked many and they wanted to surrender immediately. However, Collins' ordered his men to keep moving and let the rear echelon units round the prisoners up. The plan to advance quickly under cover of darkness was a complete success; it had taken the Germans completely by surprise. Under cover of darkness, the column of tanks and halftracks moved swiftly through Vettelhovgen and Bolingen, towards Lantershofen. 60th Armored Infantry Battalion eventually reached his objective at 2:00 am, where Lieutenant-Colonel Collins was able to let his men dig in and rest while the rest of the division completed its advance to the Rhine.

Overnight in Remagen

As CCB advanced towards Meckenheim, eight miles to the east, in Remagen, *Hauptmann* Bratge's concerns were growing. Although the bridge was closed to wheeled traffic while engineers boarded over the tracks, foot soldiers had continued to cross the bridge throughout the day. They brought news that American troops were close behind and it appeared that there were no organised troops between them and the bridge. Bratge had seen no sign of the reinforcements promised by General Botsch and attempts to contact the General had failed. As darkness fell *Hauptmann* Bratge ordered *Feldwebel* Rothe to take the majority of his men (his company had dwindled to only thirty-six men) onto the Victoriasberg Heights to watch for signs of American troops, in the meantime he would continue to try and contact his commanding officer. Little did he know that Botsch had been transferred to command LIII Corps earlier that day without having the chance to brief his successor, *Generalmajor* Richard von Bothmer.

Although it seemed to *Hauptmann* Bratge that the Remagen crossing had been forgotten, during the early hours of 7 March

Fifteenth Army informed LXVII Corps headquarters that it had been given direct responsibility for the bridge. General Hitzfeld was told that an infantry battalion and a number of flak crews were already at Remagen and that he must send a staff officer to establish a bridgehead. Major Scheller, Hitzfeld's adjutant-general, was instructed to make his way to the town and take command of the troops already there, bolstering their numbers with any stragglers heading towards the river. He was also ordered to oversee the engineers' work as they prepared the bridge for demolition. Just before 03:00 Major Scheller accompanied by *Hauptmann* Vasel, eight men

General Otto Maximilian Hitzfeld.

and a radio, drove off into the darkness on the start of their long journey. It would take them nearly eight hours to navigate their way through the crowds of men and vehicles jamming the roads.

With the Americans closing in on the Rhine, Major Hans Scheller was ordered to Remagen take command at the bridge. Here he is pictured in happier times. Scheller/Friedensmuseum

CHAPTER FIVE

THE ADVANCE TO THE SINZIG AND REMAGEN

The Plan for 7 March

Once Brigadier-General Hoge was clear what General Leonard expected, he called together his subordinate officers. Time was running out as Hoge issued his orders and 9th Division's late change of objectives meant that the two columns would have to change their routes of advance.

The northern column, commanded by Colonel Leonard Engeman of the 14th Tank Battalion (he outranked 27th Armored Infantry Battalion's CO, Major Murray Deevers), would exit the town from the east, heading to the north of Adendorf before passing through Arzdorf and then south past Berkum. Beyond Werthoven the column would head east, bypassing Birresdorf to the north, before entering the woods covering Scheidskopf, one of the hills overlooking the Rhine. The column's final objective was the town of Remagen on the west bank of the river.

The left flank of the column would be covered by the 1st Battalion of the 310th Infantry Regiment, which would cooperate with elements of the 89th Reconnaissance Squadron. Little resistance was expected as the infantry swept the west bank of the Rhine around Bad Goesberg; the majority of the retreating German troops would be heading for the bridge at Remagen.

Lieutenant-Colonel William M Prince, 52nd Armored Infantry Battalion's commanding officer, would lead the southern column. His new objectives were as follows:

> Our mission has been changed, our mission now is to seize and secure bridgeheads over the Ahr River at Westum and Sinzig. Route of advance; Adendorf, Eckendorf, Fritzdorf, Leimersdorf, Bodendorf, Sinzig. To cross IP at southeast end of the town at 07:35. C Coy to lead to Sinzig, A Coy to follow through to take Westum, rest of battalion assemble in Bodendorf.

Time was running out as the two Colonels returned to their respective headquarters. Prince did not manage to pass on his

35

Troops of the 9th Armored Division prepare to move out. National Archives
111-SC-202353

orders until 06:45 and thirty minutes later his column of
halftracks and tanks were on the move, heading out of
Flerzheim for Stadt Meckenheim.

As CCB's staff waited for the advance to begin, a

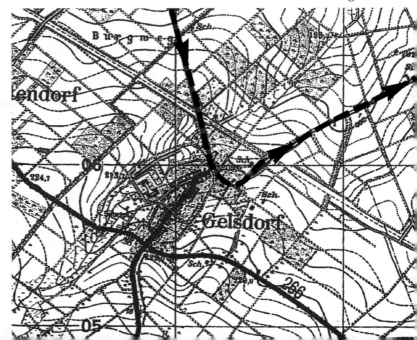

reconnaissance party returned to the headquarters having spent the night reconnoitring routes out of the town. Their findings were a cause for deep concern:

> The destruction in Stadt Meckenheim had been so thorough that there was no way for troops north and north east of the town to get through to the Adendorf road, as all the streets were completely blocked with debris. The surrounding terrain was so soggy from heavy rains that neither it nor the dirt roads leading around Stadt Meckenheim would support vehicles.

It was clear that the road assigned to the northern column was impassable to tracked vehicles. Brigadier Hoge immediately sent military policemen to the southern outskirts of the town to redirect Lieutenant-Colonel Prince's column south via Gelsdorf and Eckendorf, rejoining its prescribed route at Fritzdorf. Meanwhile, Colonel Engeman would have to leave Stadt Meckenheim via the Adendorf road once the engineers had cleared the road of rubble.

52nd Armored Infantry Battalion advances towards Sinzig

By the time the military police had reached the checkpoint, the reconnaissance vehicles scouting ahead of the southern column were already heading for Adendorf. The armoured cars came under small arms fire as they entered the village; it was however, a token gesture and the snipers quickly surrendered as

The first leg of Task Force Prince's route.

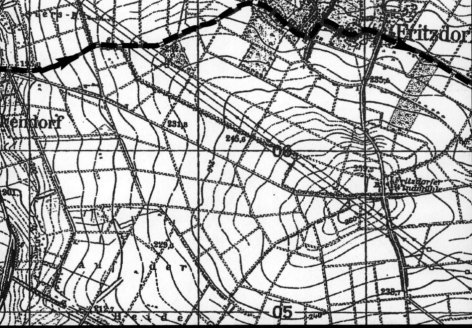

the Greyhounds returned fire.

Meanwhile, Prince's column was well under way on its new route:

> When C Company and the tanks reached the RJ [road junction] they were shunted south on the road to GELSDORF, being informed by the MP stationed there that their original route was to be used by the north column.

Progressing at a steady speed of ten miles an hour, the tanks and armoured cars were able to make good time. Open fields lined the road and although C Company halftracks approached each village with care there were no signs of German rearguards:

> The advance was virtually unopposed. As each town and village was entered, the streets would fill with people waving white flags in the effort to save their houses from destruction. In their eagerness to avoid trouble, these people freely gave information about enemy movements. The indications were that the Germans had withdrawn to the Rhine the night before.

By the time the column reached Fritzdorf, the Reconnaissance

Armoured troops advance cautiously through a German village. National Archives 111-SC-202076

element had rejoined the route and was able to begin scouting ahead. Brigadier Hoge had been carefully monitoring Prince's progress. At 09:00 he was pleased to hear that the main column had reached Oeverich while the 89th Recon Squadron had scouted as far forward as Kirchdaun. It meant that the southern column would soon be in striking distance of the River Ahr.

Few Germans had been seen along the way and although occasional rounds of mortar fire fell close by, the column kept moving. It appeared that the majority of German troops had already escaped across the Rhine the previous night and Brigadier Hoge was sure that the overnight delay in Meckenheim had let the opportunity to capture large numbers of the enemy slip away.

Beyond Kirchdaun the column came to an abrupt halt as the lead platoon's halftracks and supporting tanks floundered in thick mud. Rather than wait for his men to extricate their vehicles, Lieutenant-Colonel Prince decided to reroute the rest of the column through Gimmigen to the south. The trapped

The southern column advanced quickly towards Sinzig. Natio

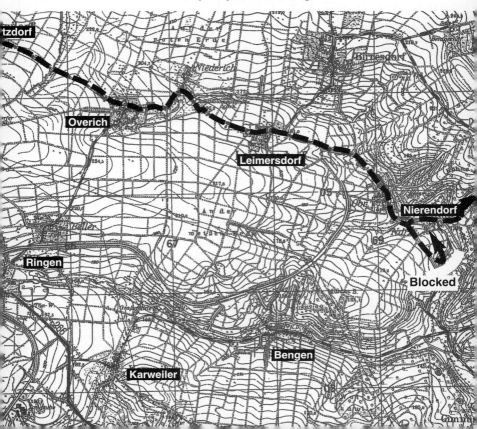

52 Armored Infantry Battalion managed to capture the bridge over the River Ahr intact.

vehicles would have to rejoin the advance once they had freed themselves.

Forty-five minutes were lost as the column struggled to reorganise itself and after passing through Gimmigen, 52nd Armored Infantry Battalion came under observed fire for the first time that morning. A German rearguard occupying a church overlooking the road targeted Prince's men with accurate small arms and mortar fire:

> *Company C and Company A were waved on through to allow the tank destroyers and assault guns from Headquarters Company to come up into a position from which they could blast out the enemy strongpoint. The church and an adjacent structure were razed. The third platoon of Company B was then sent up to*

clean out the wreckage. The platoon took two prisoners and found six enemy dead.

Following the brief gun battle, the 52nd Armored Infantry Battalion resumed its journey, heading through Heppingen and Bodendorf heading towards the final objective, Sinzig.

Lieutenant-Colonel Prince expected the Germans to defend the town and the bridge over the River Ahr. He ordered Company C and the tanks attached to his command, to approach the town with care, while Company A followed in support. As the lead halftracks drew near mortar fire, directed from the high ground across the river began to target them. As the infantry dismounted, they came under machine gunfire from concrete emplacements guarding the two roads into the town. German infantry, hidden in slit trenches and log bunkers, soon joined in the battle. The combined firepower of the Shermans' 75mm guns and the 0.05 calibre machine guns quickly overwhelmed the rearguard, allowing Company C to push on into the town.

German engineers tried to blow up the main bridge as the halftracks approached but the demolition charges failed to destroy the structure. As Company C dismounted to begin

German rearguards were quickly dealt with en route to Sinzig. National Archives 111-SC-203182

clearing the north bank of the river, Company A crossed the damaged bridge and headed towards Westrum. As Prince's men fanned out through the town, the Germans tried to escape towards Kripp, in the hope of reaching the ferry at Linz. For the majority it was too late:

> Just inside the town Company C ran into an enemy ammunition train consisting of about twelve trucks and horse drawn vehicles. This column was completely smashed with small arms fire and machine gun fire, all enemy personnel with the train being killed either by fire or by the exploding ammunition.

Captain Wortham's men eventually captured over three hundred prisoners, many of them wounded left behind during the retreat.

Lieutenant-Colonel Price had managed to take all his objectives by 13:00 and later on he was able to report that seventy-five of the enemy had been killed and over four hundred men had been taken prisoner. His own casualties were minimal.

27th Armored Infantry Battalion's advance on Remagen

As the southern column raced towards its objective, Colonel Engeman was still waiting for the engineers to clear a route out of Meckenheim. Although tanks fitted with bulldozer blades helped to clear the rubble from the main street, 27th Armored Infantry Battalion had to wait for two hours they could move. Brigadier

Hoge was frustrated by the delay, convinced that the Germans were escaping across the Rhine at Remagen.

Eventually at 09:00 the platoon of armoured cars from the 89th Reconnaissance Squadron headed off towards Adendorf. Company A, under Lieutenant Karl Timmermann, led the main column and for Timmermann leading a company was a new experience; the previous day Captain Kriner had been wounded in the attack on Meckenheim. Pershing tanks,

Lieutenant Karl Timmermann.
National Archives 111-SC-202343

The new M26 Pershing tank was armed with a powerful 90mm gun. National Archives 111-SC-455227

under Captain George Soumas, were interspersed between the halftracks.

Although reconnaissance vehicles had previously passed through Adendorf, as soon as the column entered the village it came under small arms fire. Moving slowly forward, the tanks and halftracks targeted any signs of movement with their machine guns while the GIs watched for snipers. However, the Germans only intended to put up a token resistance and as soon

The first stage of Task Force Engeman's route.

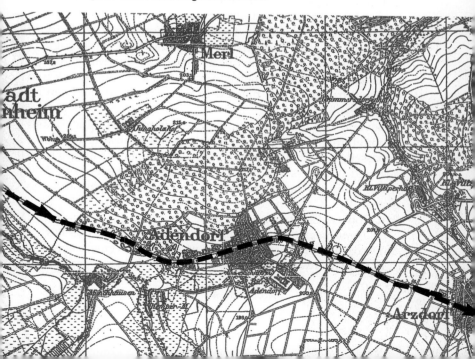

as the armoured column drew near the 27th Armored Infantry Battalion was over-whelmed with prisoners. Already behind schedule, the head of the column pushed on, leaving the prisoners behind for the support troops to deal with. Later interrogation revealed that the majority of the Fifth *Panzer* Army Group's Storm Battalion had capitulated en masse along with the crew of a heavy anti-aircraft battery.

As the column left Adendorf machine gun fire to the north brought the column to a halt until it was identified that friendly troops were engaging an enemy rearguard. As the head of the column crossed open fields on the approach to Arzdorf, the lead halftrack noticed a barricade blocking the road and opened fire with its 0.5 machine gun. The rest of the halftracks joined in, spraying the houses either side of the road with bullets as machine guns and *Panzerfausts* returned fire from woods north of the road. Lieutenant Timmermann ordered his men to dismount and split his company in two, to outflank the village. As the GIs crept forward through the fields either side of the road, the halftracks and tanks moved slowly towards the outskirts of Arzdorf, providing covering fire. Before long a handful of young soldiers emerged with their hands up; another German rearguard had capitulated. As Timmermann watched his men climb back into their halftracks he was pleased to hear that there had been no casualties.

Beyond Arzdorf the column was able to move quickly and although there were tense moments as the halftracks and tanks bypassed Berkum and through Werthhoven, both villages were deserted. Villagers had hung white flags and sheets from their windows in the hope that the Americans would pass through peacefully. Captain Soumas, commander of 14th Tank Battalion's A Company noted that:

> *Throughout the movement, very little opposition was met. The column was constantly being passed by little groups of two or three prisoners marching to the rear, hands behind heads, to*

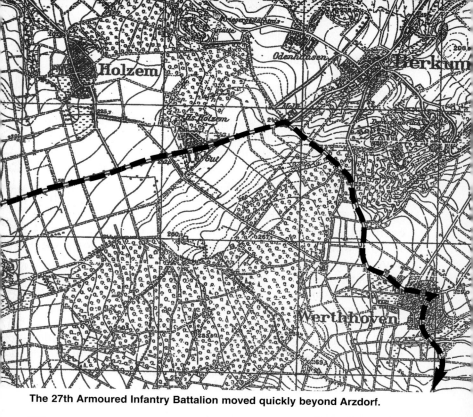

The 27th Armoured Infantry Battalion moved quickly beyond Arzdorf.

Villagers display a white flag to show that German troops have already fled.
National Archives 111-SC-203183

give themselves up to the nearest authority willing to accept their surrender.

Colonel Engeman also recalled that resistance along the route was minimal:

> *Small arms, fire of a scattered nature, light artillery and a little AAA fire were all that was encountered on the advance towards the Rhine River and there were very few casualties.*

Can the Bridge be taken intact?

While the two columns snaked their way across the rolling countryside towards the Rhine, a single Piper Cub was circling overhead. Lieutenant Harold E Larsen and Lieutenant Frank L Vaughn were on a reconnaissance flight, the first for several days due to poor weather.

> *Their mission was to find passable roads and bridges, enemy dispositions and to fire any artillery targets that might appear... They were given the additional mission of trying to see whether the bridge over the Rhine at REMAGEN was intact.*

Having covered the skies over the two columns, Larsen decided to risk flying towards Remagen even though low clouds meant that he would have to fly well within the effective range of active anti-aircraft batteries. The gamble paid off. Although

The German view of the Ludendorff Bridge, barbed wire entanglements line the railway. National Archives 111-SC-202786

Larsen saw crowds of troops and vehicles heading for the river, no one seemed to take notice of the plane overhead:

> As the columns approached the Rhine River, Lt Larsen flew on ahead towards the river in order to look over the area. He was able to see the outline of a bridge, but was unable to tell whether the structure was capable of carrying traffic. Knowing that such a structure would be well guarded with flak batteries, Lt Larsen did not deviate from his plan to make a reconnaissance of the bridge.

Lieutenant Larsen radioed the news back to 16th Armored Field Artillery Battalion headquarters and Colonel Wesner immediately passed on the information to Combat Command B. The time was 10:30 when Hoge first learnt that the Remagen Bridge was still intact.

Colonel Engeman's column was still several hours behind schedule and more than seven miles from the town. Although he had not been given any written instructions, Hoge had no doubt what he should do. The subject of the Ludendorff Bridge had been raised earlier that morning when Major-General Leonard visited CCB headquarters. Brigadier Hoge later remarked how he had posed the question:

> I drew a line around the bridge on my map and asked General Leonard, Suppose I find that the bridge hasn't been blown here, should I take it?

Leonard had left Hoge in no doubt; the bridge should be taken.

Major Ben Cothran, Hoge's intelligence officer, was ordered to catch up with the head of the northern column to pass on the news about the bridge as well as instil a sense of urgency in Colonel Engeman. As the S3 officer left in his jeep, Hoge set off to find Lieutenant-Colonel Prince, to oversee the crossing of the River Ahr. Deep down he expected that the Germans would destroy the bridge as soon as their troops had crossed.

Crisis at the Bridge

While the two columns of Combat Command B moved steadily towards the Rhine, German troops continued to escape across the river. For the past twenty-four hours foot troops, in particular the shattered 277th Volksgrenadier Division (reduced to around 800 men), had been crossing the Ludendorff Bridge. As the soldiers trudged through the town their faces left no doubt in the minds of the local population that the German Army was in the middle of a full-scale retreat. The following day Remagen's Chief of Police told an American intelligence officer: '...the officers left three days ago, the NCOs left yesterday and the privates must swim.'

Although foot troops had been able to cross the bridge for the past four days it had been closed to wheeled traffic while engineers placed timber decking over the rail tracks to allow armour to cross. The closure had led to a build of traffic in the streets and by the time the bridge opened at first light on 7 March there was a considerable build up of traffic. Rumours that American armoured columns had been spotted advancing towards the town added a sense of urgency and the sounds of gunfire to the south as 52nd Armoured Infantry Battalion attacked Sinzig confirmed the reports. As the soldiers waiting their turn to cross the river watching the hills overlooking Remagen for signs of American troops, the endless column of supply wagons, lorries and tanks made their way over the bridge:

On 6 and 7 March large numbers of the 277 Volksgrenadier

Infantry deploy into the fields while tanks engage a German strongpoint.
National Archives 111-SC-201898

Division crossed. They had a considerable number of horses but no artillery. Some armour also crossed in the same period, including 3 Tiger Royal, 20 Mark IV and 2 SP guns.

Amongst the column of vehicles were a number of flak batteries and their crews. They were the men who were supposed to assist the bridge security company in an emergency but despite Captain Bratge's protests the officer in charge of the guns was adamant that he was acting under orders. It left Bratge with his small company of men to defend the bridge and the majority were already stationed on Victoriasberg Heights.

As the hours passed, Bratge's attempts to get men to stay on the west bank to defend the town failed. The majority were stragglers without officers and there only concern was to cross the Rhine at the first opportunity. Rumours that an armoured column had been spotted heading for Birresdorf only four miles away only made them more determined to escape across the river. When Bratge contacted Army Group B Headquarters to report the news he was assured that the Americans were heading for Bonn.

Some time after 10:00 Major Scheller eventually reached Remagen, having spent all night on the road. After informing Bratge that he was the new 'Commandant of Remagen', the two officers assessed the situation. Scheller had expected to find a battalion of troops waiting for him at Remagen, ready to form a defensive perimeter around the town with the flak crews stationed in the area. Meanwhile, Bratge had heard nothing of the reinforcements promised by General Botsch and he also informed Scheller that the flak batteries had already withdrawn to the east bank. His own company was already in position on the Victoriasberg heights, leaving only a handful of men to guard the bridge. Although Major Scheller approved the withdrawal of the company to defend the bridge, attempts to contact them failed. In the meantime Scheller's tried to get men to stay on the west bank and defend the bridge. Although he eventually managed to get a machine gun team to stop as soon as he turned his back the men disappeared.

Meanwhile, Captain Friesenhahn had taken steps to prepare the bridge for demolition. He had sent transport to collect the explosives, which until now, had been stored in a safe place away from the bridge. The lorry carrying the explosives eventually arrived at around 11:00 but to Friesenhahn's dismay the amount delivered was far less than expected. Although he had the full compliment of packages required for the primary circuits, the amount sent for the emergency charges was less that expected. He had requested six hundred kilograms of military explosive, but the quantity sent was less than half of that and the charges were a weaker industrial grade, not the standard military issue. Despite the setback, Friesenhahn had no time to argue; all he could do was order his men to distribute the charges at the weakest points on the bridge.

Over the next three hours his men worked feverishly to install over four hundred pounds of explosive charges in the metal boxes fixed to the bridge girders. The plan was to cut all the trusses on the downstream side, sending the main span toppling sideways into the river. Further charges would break the back of the two smaller spans sending them crashing into the water. Once his men had placed all the charges connected to the primary circuit, they started to stack the remaining packages above the upstream pier. If the main circuitry failed Friesenhahn would be able to use primer cords would be used to detonate them. Although the engineers worked continuously throughout the morning, extracts from the 9th Armored Engineer Battalion's report shows how little time they had:

The final leg of the northern column as it approached Remagen.

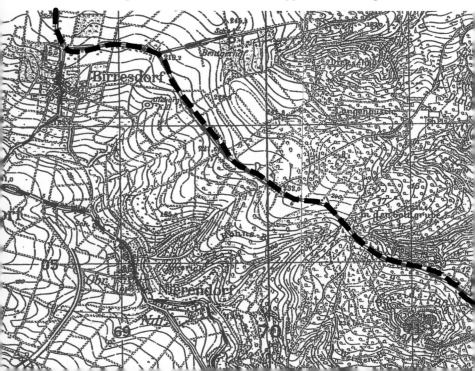

There was an estimated 600lbs of TNT on all the members [above the far stream pier]. The charges were packed in cardboard boxes whose exact dimensions are unknown. They appear to be hastily placed and were to be exploded with time fuze and a non-electric cap... Various charges were also scattered on the far shore span, the location of which cannot be determined. These appear to have been placed in great haste and seemingly without scheme or plan.

27th Armored Infantry Battalion continue to push east

While Major Cothran raced across the countryside to catch up with Colonel Engeman, the head of the northern column had bypassed Birresdorf and was heading east towards the wooded slopes of the Scheidskopf:

Mortar fire off road east of Objective 1 – Head of column 1,400 yards east of Birresdorf. Preparing to enter woods and assault final objective. Recon in front of Rebel. Good pace beyond Birresdorf, no enemy resistance.

However, Engeman had spoken too soon. As A Company approached the tree line shots rang out as a German rearguard engaged the column with small arms fire. Although Lieutenant Timmermann ordered his men to dismount within minutes the Germans emerged from the woods with their hands up.

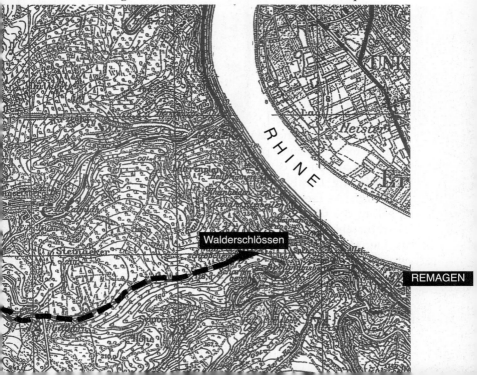

As the column entered the woods, the GIs stared intently into the trees looking for signs of activity; it was the perfect place for an ambush. The sound of the halftracks and tanks echoing through the woods convinced some German soldiers to give themselves up, while the rest hid. The lack of German resistance was a relief to Colonel Engeman; thick woods and steep sided slopes would have made it difficult to engage a determined enemy.

Plattborn, a cluster of houses nestling in the trees, was deserted and as the column began to descend through the woods towards the Rhine, Major Cothran caught up the tail of the column. The news about the bridge was quickly transmitted to Colonel

Engeman by radio and he was able to confirm to Brigadier Hoge that the reconnaissance platoon was closing in on Remagen.

As the armoured column approached Waldeschlössen tavern the Allmang family watched silently while waving a white tablecloth. As Lieutenant Timmermann pulled up in his jeep to speak to the family, the halftracks and tanks rumbled past. A short distance beyond the tavern the trees began to thin out and as Lieutenant Emmett Burrows' platoon emerged from the woods they were taken aback by an astonishing panorama. In the valley below the Rhine wound its way past Remagen and

'Hey Tim, take a look at that!' The bridge was still intact.

although Erpeler Ley, the huge rocky outcrop on the far bank of the river, dominated the horizon, Lieutenant Burrows' eyes were focussed on the Ludendorff Railway Bridge at the foot of the crag. Through his binoculars he could see that traffic was crossing the river:

> *The enemy was retreating with trucks and smaller vehicles* (no armour was observed) *and there were many civilians mixed in with the military traffic.*

It meant that the Germans had not destroyed the bridge.

Lieutenant Timmermann was called forward and as he approached Burrows shouted, 'Hey, Tim, take a look at that'!

'Dammit, that's the Rhine; I didn't think it was that close.' Timmermann replied.

Upon the news of the intact bridge, Colonel Engeman and Major Deevers raced to the head of the column to see for themselves. The report reads:

Their first reaction was to try and get artillery fire brought down on enemy vehicles which were clearly seen crossing the bridge. The forward observer of the 400th Armored Field Artillery Battalion was called up, and he was highly elated at the possible opportunity to employ his new pozit fuse. However, higher authorities refused permission, stating that friendly troops were on or in the vicinity of the bridge.

After contacting Brigadier Hoge, Colonel Engeman was ordered to prepare to enter the town as soon as possible. In the meantime Hoge would make his way to the viewpoint to see the spectacle for himself. As Engeman wryly noted later:

At that time I smelled that they wanted to take the bridge intact... Although the mission was still to take and occupy REMAGEN and KRIPP, there was still in the back of our heads the thought with which we had started that morning – that it might be possible to seize the bridge.

CHAPTER SIX

THE ADVANCE INTO REMAGEN

Evacuation of Remagen

As Colonel Engeman's troops prepared to advance down the slopes into Remagen, the German commanders, Major Scheller and *Hauptmann* Bratge were resigned to the fact that they would have to withdraw across the river. There was no time to contact the Bridge Security Company and the reinforcements promised by Fifteenth Army had failed to materialise. *Hauptmann* Freisenhahn's men were fully employed preparing the bridge for demolition and the crews of the flak guns had already been directed elsewhere. Although men from the 277th *Volksgrenadier* Division had been making their way through the town all that morning, the two officers had been able to stop them. Major Scheller's orders to establish a bridgehead on the west bank were impossible to carry out.

Major Scheller.

Around noon an artillery officer from 277th *Volksgrenadier* Division contacted Scheller. The division had four artillery regiments and the three motorised regiments had already crossed the Rhine upstream. However, the remaining horse drawn regiment had been cut off from the rest by the American advance and was now heading for Remagen. The officer was concerned that the bridge would be destroyed before it reached the town. Scheller reassured him the bridge would be kept open until the very last moment.

An hour later the rumours that the Americans were close were confirmed when they were sighted on the hill above Apollinaris Church. Time was running out and as the engineers hurried to complete their work, Major Scheller ordered *Hauptmann* Bratge to cross the bridge and re-establish his headquarters on the east bank of the river. The American troops on the hill seemed to have halted, it was only a matter of time

Sergeant Malcolm Fleming admires the view over the Apollinaris Church and the Rhine. National Archives 111-SC-377909

before began their advance into Remagen town itself. In the meantime, Scheller decided to wait behind on the west bank for the missing artillery regiment.

Advance into Remagen

It was a few minutes before 13:00 when US troops first looked down on the Ludendorff Bridge. As Colonel Engeman and Major Deevers considered their next move lieutenants Timmermann and William McMasters reconnoitred possible routes into the town. Infantry could advance down the steep slopes past the Apollinaris Church on foot, however, vehicles

Ludendorff
Bridge

Soumas' Tanks

erman's Infantry

pollinaris Church

were restricted to the road, which wound down the hillside into the town.

Engeman considered sending all the infantry into the town mounted in halftracks, and 'take the road shooting', however, the plan was rejected in case they ran into strong German rearguards. Instead he chose to send Lieutenant Timmermann's company down the hill on foot, setting off at 14:00. Twenty minutes later Lieutenant John Grimball's platoon of Pershing tanks would:

> ...barrel down the hill and go through and cover the bridge with tank fire, and if anyone attempted to repair or demolish the bridge to liquidate them.

Company C, under Lieutenant McMasters, would follow the tanks mounted in their halftracks. It was hoped that the foot soldiers and the armour would reach the outskirts of the town simultaneously.

Once Lieutenant Timmermann had given the signal to advance, Lieutenant Burrows led 2nd Platoon down the hill, while Sergeant Joe DeLisio and Sergeant Michael Chinchar echeloned their platoons behind his flanks. Although it appeared as though the Germans had fled, the GIs kept a lookout for snipers who might have stayed. Twenty minutes later the Pershing tanks began moving down the road and although they saw no signs of enemy activity they encountered a crater at the bottom of the hill. Sergeant Grimball voiced his concern that it could be a trap and was reluctant to continue. Colonel Engeman's reply left no doubt what he should do, 'never mind the crater, get going toward the bridge'.

Meanwhile, *Feldwebel* Rothe was still at the Waldberg Hotel, waiting for instructions from *Hauptmann* Bratge. Despite the fact that there had been no signs of American troops on the Victoriasberg Heights, as soon as he saw Company A moving down the slopes past the Apollinaris Church, he knew he had to contact his officer. Attempts to call his headquarters failed and there was no time to gather up his men from the outposts half a mile to the west. All Rothe could do was to run down the hill into the town and raise the alarm.

As Company A entered Remagen, the Pershings turned right to bypass the town centre. Brigadier Hoge arrived on the heights and made it clear to Engeman what he expected, 'I want you to get to the bridge as soon as possible'.

Engeman's was equally enthusiastic, 'I am doing every damn thing possible to get to the bridge'.

Down in the town Timmermann's men were cautiously making their way along Marktstrasse past the town hall. There were no immediate signs of armed resistance, but the narrow street was ideal for an ambush. Dodging from doorway to doorway, the GIs edged forward as the local population looked on anxiously. Lieutenant Timmermann later recalled how the townspeople watched silently as the young soldiers passed by:

Many people had white flags out already, and some stood in

Infantry make their way along Marktstrasse towards the bridge. National Archives 111-SC-201876-1

the street waving white flags. None of the civilians appeared happy or cheered; many of them wept. The three platoons of Company A leapfrogged each other as they proceeded through the town of REMAGEN, cleaning it out house by house.

Although the advance was proceeding according to plan, Brigadier Hoge and Colonel Engeman were still concerned that the Germans might try and blow up the bridge at the last moment. As Sergeant Grimball drove past the town he was able to confirm that the majority of Germans had fled,

Bring all big boys and assault guns up. Proceeding to bridge – town looks deserted only 10 to 12 soldiers out posting bridge, receiving some fire now don't know what it will amount to.

As the Pershings drew closer to the approach ramps the tank crews noticed a train making steam on the far bank. The opportunity was too good to miss,

Because of their relative positions, machine gun fire could not be brought to bear on the locomotive, so 90mm was used. The locomotive was about 800 yards south of the bridge, and had a long string of flat cars and some boxcars behind it. It had scarcely got under way when the first round from Sergeant Shaeffer's tank ripped into it at a vital point, immobilising it. The next round knocked out an enemy truck which happened to be passing right in front of the locomotive on a parallel road.

Despite Grimball's assurances that he was closing in on the bridge, Brigadier Hoge ordered Colonel Engeman to catch up with his tanks and take control of the situation. As Engeman drove down into the town he radioed Grimball, urging him to get as quickly to the bridge as possible, 'I am at the bridge' came the reply. 'All right, cover the bridge with fire and don't let the Krauts do any more work on it.'

While Timmermann and Grimball were making their way towards the bridge, *Hauptmann* Friesenhahn had been put the finishing touches to his work. After ordering all but two his men to retire across the bridge Friesenhahn waited to detonate the explosives dug into the approach ramp to create an anti-tank trench. Before long, the three men could hear the rumble of tanks through the streets. Time was running out and after ordering his two guards to withdraw, Friesenhahn pressed the plunger, the time was 15:12,

His [Timmermann's] small force headed straight for the bridge, the tanks leading. Just as they arrived at the earth ramp *leading onto the bridge the first charge exploded, leaving a large crater in the runway.*

The explosion had torn a gouge in the approach ramp three metres deep and ten metres wide, stopping the tanks driving onto the bridge.

As Company A closed in, *Hauptmann* Friesenhahn began to run across the bridge as the sound of gunfire echoed around the valley. One shell exploded close to the girderwork concussing Friesenhahn and, as he lay unconscious, another German soldier staggered onto the bridge. *Feldwebel* Rothe had managed to run down the hill from the Waldberg Hotel without being seen. Lieutenant Timmermann later recalled what happened when his men spotted Rothe:

> *One German Luftwaffe sergeant refused to stop when called upon, so he was shot through the groin. Otherwise, there was no firing until close to the bridge when enemy machine gunners sent a few rounds from the towers on the bridge. No casualties resulted.*

Hauptmann Friesenhahn and Feldwebel Rothe eventually managed to reach the east bank of the river and, although dazed, Friesenhahn went in search of Major Scheller. Everything was in place to destroy the bridge, but it was Scheller who had to give the order to detonate the charges.

Build up at the bridge

In the meantime the rest of Task Force Engeman was making its way towards the bridge. Sergeant Grimball had stationed one Pershing on the approach road, covering the railway tracks; the other three were lined along the road firing at targets on the east bank. Company A's first attempt to advance onto the approach ramps had been met by heavy fire from AA guns on the far bank. While the tanks dealt with the guns Company A regrouped for a second attempt.

Meanwhile, Company C was making its way through Remagen. Lieutenant McMasters had split his halftracks into three groups, each consisting of four of five halftracks and while one group made its way through the centre of the town, a second group made its way along the promenade. The third group followed Grimball's Pershings along the bypass. Colonel Engeman had also ordered the rest of Company A's tanks, nine Shermans, to head towards the bridge at top speed. When the

Shermans arrived they lined up alongside the Pershings at fifty-yard intervals.

While Colonel Engeman was preparing to cross the bridge, a report over his radio introduced a degree of urgency into his task. The reports are confusing, but it would seem that at around 15:15 Brigadier Hoge received disturbing news. Men of 89th Reconnaissance Squadron had rounded up two civilians in Sinzig as they searched the town for German soldiers. The two men informed Lieutenant DeRange, 52nd Armored Infantry Battalion's intelligence officer, that the Ludendorff Bridge was due to be destroyed at 16:00. The accuracy of the information was doubtful but it did put Brigadier Hoge in a dilemma. Although he had men at the bridge his tanks were unable to cross due to the preliminary explosion that had damaged the approaches.

Brigadier Hoge recalls his reaction to the news,

> At 15:15 on 7 March – that's the only specific time during this operation of which I am certain – we received a PW [prisoner of war] report that the bridge was to be blown at 16:00. I immediately told Col Engeman that he had 45 minutes before the bridge was likely to be blown, and advised him to put WP [White Phosphorous] and smoke around the area, and cautioned him to cover his advance with tanks and machine guns, bring up his engineers to pull firing wires and whatever fuses found, and make a dash across the bridge.

With little time to spare, Colonel Engeman gave the order to cross. However, as the men of Company A prepared themselves

American engineers study the damage caused by the German demolition explosion. National Archives 111-SC-323975

there was a huge explosion across the river.

Forty-five minutes passed before *Hauptmann* Friesenhahn managed to locate Major Scheller and after a brief argument over responsibilities, he was finally given the written order he wanted. After giving a warning, Friesenhahn turned the ignition switch for the primary circuit. Nothing happened. Several more attempts proved that the circuitry had been damaged. Whether it was the result of enemy fire or sabotage will never be known. Brigadier Hoge later explained his own theory in his After-Action report:

> *After careful investigation of all reports on why the bridge was not blown this headquarters believes that a Polish railroad worker at Erpel, one Sivinski, cut the wires and tied them back so that the cut could not be detected by inspection.*

Another explanation could be that during the delay looking for Major Scheller, shrapnel had severed the cabling. Whatever the reason, the only option left for the officers at the eastern end of the bridge was to detonate the emergency charges.

In response to Hauptmann Friesenhahn's calls for volunteers, *Feldwebel* Anton Faust led a handful of men back onto the bridge to detonate the secondary charges.

After lighting the primer cords, they returned to the safety of the tunnel to escape the huge explosion that proceeded to rock the construction along its length. All eyes turned expecting to watch as the Ludendorff Bridge fell into the river. When the dust and smoke cleared German and American soldiers alike, were astonished to see that the structure was still standing. One American engineer report read,

> *The charges upstream detonated and severed several members [girders]. On the downstream charge the cap exploded and the primer block shattered and neighbouring blocks [were] disturbed but the charge did not explode.*

CHAPTER SEVEN

ACROSS THE RHINE

Crossing the Bridge

As the noise of the explosion echoed around the valley, Lieutenant Timmermann called out, 'as you were, we can't cross the bridge now because it has just been blown'. Yet as the smoke cleared Company A were astonished to see that the bridge was still standing. The charges had sheared a number of girders supporting the upstream truss above the far pier. They had also destroyed a large section of timber decking, leaving a gaping hole in the floor of the bridge two-thirds the way across the river.

As the clouds of dust cleared Lieutenant Timmermann could see that his men could still cross with care and called out, 'we'll cross the bridge – order of march 1st Platoon, 3rd Platoon and 2nd Platoon'. He intended to have his only remaining officer, Lieutenant Burrows, cross at the rear of the column. As the

The damage caused to the bridge girders above the bridge pier can be clearly seen. National Archives 111-SC-203739

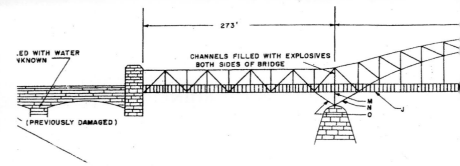

The Ludendorff Bridge, the charges were stacked over the pier to the right.

company prepared to move out, Colonel Engeman had taken steps to cover their advance with smoke. The tank destroyers and 105mm assault guns attached to his task force were lined up on the hill above Apollinaris Church and began firing white phosphorous shells. 27th Armored Infantry Battalion's mortar platoon joined in, creating an acrid screen of smoke that drifted across the valley.

As 1st Platoon filed up the approach ramp, Sergeant Anthony Samele turned to his platoon leader, Sergeant Michael Chinchar, and gave a few words of encouragement: 'C'mon, Mike, we'll just walk it over.' Chinchar set off half running, half crouching, onto the viaduct followed by Private Art Massie and an officer of the 9th Armored Engineer Battalion, Lieutenant Mott. Samele came close behind and he may have heard Major Deevers' jest; 'I'll see you on the other side and we'll all have chicken dinner.'

As 1st Platoon made their way onto the bridge, 3rd Platoon, led by Sergeant Joe DeLisio, gave covering fire while the Germans on the far bank returned fire. When Sergeant Chinchar reached the first pair of bridge towers he ordered Private Massie to lead some of the platoon onto the bridge. 'Massie, you leapfrog me up as far as that blown hole.' Massie's replied, 'I don't want to go but I will'. The rest of Chinchar's men entered the towers to make sure they were clear of German soldiers. As the GIs ducked and weaved along the timber walkway, bullets and shells ricocheted of the bridge girders:

> Sniper fire rattled around the bridge, along with some 20mm fire from the high ground on the south bank near REMAGEN, also a few rounds of high velocity fire hit the superstructure of the bridge.

Although the first two towers on the west bank were unoccupied, the matching towers on the opposite bank were obviously manned. Machine guns stationed in the upper storey

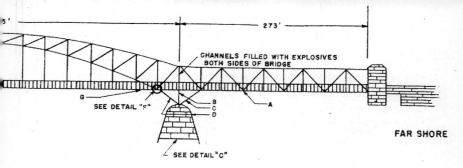

CHANNELS FILLED WITH EXPLOSIVES
BOTH SIDES OF BRIDGE

SEE DETAIL "ᶠ"

G

B
C
D

A

FAR SHORE

SEE DETAIL "C"

windows were firing furiously sending streams of bullets over the heads of Timmermann's men as they filed across the centre span. The crackle of fire coming from the enemy-held bank sounded impressive, but Company A suffered no casualties. The Germans in the towers were finding it difficult to find targets through the lattice of bridge girders.

At the same time as Chinchar's men made there way past the hole in the decking above the second pier, Lieutenant Mott and his two assistants had begun to search for the detonation wiring. They hoped to cut it in case the Germans somehow still had the means to blow the bridge. Lieutenant Mott soon found the metal tubing carrying the cable for the primary charges and placed the muzzle of his gun against the pipe. He fired three shots, blasting open the conduit and severing the cable, thus rendering the circuitry useless.

As Timmermann's men made their way towards the far bank some wondered if the Germans had machine guns waiting in railway tunnel ahead. If they had opened fire at the last minute, Company A would be decimated. Major Deevers later commented how he 'was worried more than anything else about guns in that tunnel'.

As Sergeant DeLisio's platoon made their way past the hole in the decking, anyone who cared to look down would have seen the swirling waters of the Rhine ten metres below. Firing as they ran, 1st Platoon began to get ever closer to the towers on the far bank. Despite the fact that just about every German unit in the vicinity was firing everything they had at the bridge, so far only one man had been slightly wounded:

A small amount of artillery was coming in [maybe it was mortar fire], *along with sniper fire, and some anti-aircraft fire, from the south side along the high ground on the near bank.*

At last Sergeant DeLisio reached the foot of the right hand tower and smashed his way through the door. The office beyond was empty. As he climbed the spiral staircase, gun at the ready, he could hear the sound of automatic fire coming from above. Moments later the gunfire stopped and as DeLisio burst into the next room he was confronted by three German soldiers huddled over their weapon. A couple of warning shots encouraged the gun crew to put their hands up. Motioning the crew away from the weapon he tipped it out of the window. He asked as best he could about any others in the tower. They assured him that they were the only men in the building, however, DeLisio decided to check out the top floor. Sending his captives ahead of him up the stairs he followed close behind. On the next floor he discovered a further two Germans, an officer and his orderly. A warning shot encouraged their surrender.

Meanwhile, Sergeant Chinchar led two men into the left hand tower. Here they captured a solitary German who had been manning a machine gun at an upper storey window. After tossing the weapon to the ground below, Chinchar shouted down to his men, giving them the all clear.

Sergeant Alex Drabik – the first man across the Rhine. National Archives 111-SC-202534

While the lead men had been tackling the towers others continued to run across towards the east bank:

Sergeant Alex Drabik came up and barrelled across the bridge to win the honour of being the first man across, although no one was thinking of that at the time. Just as he got across, Sgt Drabik stumbled and fell and lost his helmet, which Brigadier-General William C Hoge later picked up.

Company A establish a toehold on the east bank

The first American soldiers set foot on the east bank of the River Rhine a few minutes after 16:00 hours 7 March, 1945. Sergeant Drabik was unaware that Sergeant DeLisio was still engaged in the bridge tower and, after rounding up a few men, he turned left, heading along the riverbank looking for his platoon leader. After two hundred metres, it was obvious that there were no other American soldiers up ahead so Drabik established a firing line in shell craters straddling the railway line. Chinchar's platoon headed in the opposite direction and established a defensive line at the foot of the Erpeler Ley. Lieutenant Burrows platoon brought up the rear of Company A and joined Drabik north of the bridge. Burrows was the first US Army officer to step foot on the east bank of the river Rhine. By now there were seventy men holding a tight perimeter either side of the bridge.

Once Lieutenant Timmermann had crossed, his main concern was that the Germans could counterattack from the railway tunnel into the centre of A Company's position. Sergeant DeLisio had just returned from the bridge tower and he was ordered to take four men to investigate the tunnel. As DeLisio moved cautiously along the rail tracks the bend in the tunnel made it difficult to see what lay ahead. As their eyes became accustomed to the darkness the GIs saw shadowy figures in the distance. After firing a single shot, four of Friesenhahn's engineers raised their hands and stepped forward. Once he had reached the bend in the tunnel Sergeant DeLisio could see that the rest of the tunnel was deserted. Although there were civilians in the cutting beyond the tunnel, they did not pose a threat to Company A's position and DeLisio was able to return to report his findings.

As Brigadier Hoge watched Company A cross the bridge from the hill above Remagen, new orders came through from divisional headquarters. Major-General Leonard wanted CCB to push south in the hope of cutting off German troops retiring to the Rhine. The instructions presented Hoge with a dilemma. If he was to have a chance of maintaining a foothold he needed to keep pushing men across the river into the established bridgehead. Although Brigadier Hoge needed confirmation from Leonard as quickly as possible, he decided to keep on sending his men across the bridge. The message dictated by Hoge at 16:18 would soon be repeated all the way up to the top of the Allied chain of command:

We have a bridge intact across the river at Checkpoint 15 [Remagen]. *Shall I continue to hold this bridgehead in view of the new mission south? We have one company across at 16:10.*

In order to clarify the order, Hoge immediately set off back

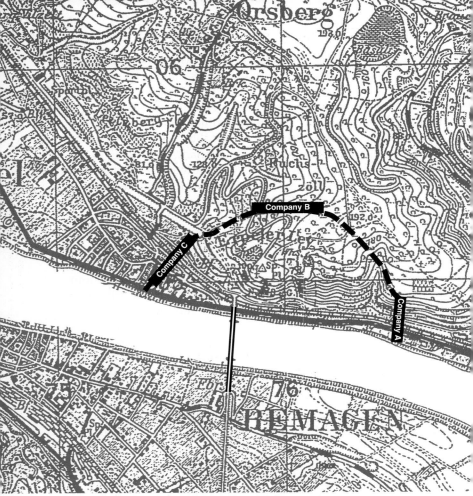

27th Armoured Infantry Battalion's toe hold on the east bank of the Rhine.

towards his command post in Birresdorf, leaving clear instructions with Engeman and Deevers:

> *Get demolitions off bridge and secure high ground, we will protect your rear and support you with additional troops. Dig in well on high ground and establish roadblocks well mined on east side of river.*

As Company A crossed the river and established themselves on the east bank, the German officers in charge of destroying the bridge had run through the rail tunnel. However, once on through the tunnel, *Hauptmann* Bratge and *Hauptmann*

70

MESSAGE (SUBMIT TO MESSAGE CENTER IN DUPLICATE) (CLASSIFICATION)

BBG TO G-3

No._____ DATE 7 MAR -45

To_____

WE HAVE A BRIDGE INTACT
ACROSS RIVER AT CHECK POINT
15 SHALL I CONTINUE TO
HOLD THIS BRIDGEHEAD IN
VIEW OF NEW MISSION SOUTH
WE HAVE ONE COMPANY ACROSS
RT 671610 A

Ø21618
HR

OFFICIAL DESIGNATION OF SENDER   TIME SIGNED

AUTHORIZED TO BE
SENT IN CLEAR   SIGNATURE OF OFFICER   SIGNATURE AND GRADE OF WRITER

#32

Historic message covering the crossing of the bridge.

Friesenhahn tried their best to round up men to return to contend the crossing. On the otherhand Major Scheller headed off on a bicycle, with the declared intention of reporting the news of the American success to the nearest headquarters.

27th Armored Infantry Battalion continue to cross

As Company A made their way onto the far bank of the Rhine, Company C, led by Lieutenant William E McMasters, started to cross. A Sherman, equipped with a dozer, began to fill in the crater on the approach ramp. As the tank began to level out the hole, a sniper opened fire from a partly submerged barge in the river, halting the work. The tank was unable to depress it's gun far enough to hit the barge. However, men on the bridge from Company C noticed the threat down by the river bank:

> They halted and turned their fire on the barge, where upon a sniper raised a white flag, but too late [for him].

Two 40mm flak guns on the far bank also tried to stop the engineers' work. The rest of Captain Soumas' tanks soon silenced them.

71

Troops shelter in the railway tunnel. National Archives 111-SC-201973-S

With work on the crater underway, Colonel Engeman wanted news on the state of the bridge and when Lieutenant Mott returned he was able to report that the wiring to the remaining charges had been cut. He now needed a supply of timber to repair the hole in the decking:

The bridge is OK for infantry now, and many of them are already over. We'll have it ready for vehicles in two hours.

In the meantime, his men were looking for packets of explosives, and upon finding them throwing them into the river in case a stray piece of shrapnel caused an accidental explosion.

Once Company C had crossed the bridge they made their way through Erpel to establish a defensive perimeter around the village. As McMasters' men took up positions along the railway cutting, they discovered a group of Germans hiding in the tunnel. While Timmermann's men had been filing across the bridge, the two German officers, Bratge and Friesenhahn, had rounded up a few stragglers with the intention of reaching the remaining explosives on the bridge. However, by the time they returned Company A already had the tunnel covered. As they retraced their steps, the two officers found that their escape route had been cut off, leaving them no option but to surrender.

Now that Major Deevers had secured the roads to the north and south of the bridge, his next concern was the heights dominating the crossing, Erpeler Ley. If the Germans occupied the crest they could fire down on the approach roads leading up to the bridge. B Company had brought up the rear of the 27th Armoured Infantry Battalion and after Lieutenant Jack H Liedike had assembled his men on the far bank, he was ordered to climb to the top of the cliff.

1st Platoon met up with a platoon of Company A on the outskirts of Erpel and as the two began to climb the northwest slopes of the hill, they came under heavy fire from 20mm flak

Geman infantry, manning a MG 42, shoot it out with troops on the opposite bank. Note the soldier using a rifle with a sniper scope.

guns situated on the northern edge of Erpel. The German crews had a perfect view of the hillside and as the GIs scrambled up the slopes, casualties began to mount. An entire squad of Company B was wiped out by automatic canon fire and Company A's platoon lost twelve men. The survivors pushed on, eventually finding cover beyond the crest of what become known as 'Flak Hill'.

They met the rest of Company B who had climbed the south east side of the cliff and although they had managed to remain unseen during their ascent, two men had fallen from the crag and been seriously injured. Several abandoned 20mm AA guns found at the top of the hill were destroyed and as Liedike's men took stock of their position they could see German troops in the valley above Kasbach.

At 18:00 Colonel Engeman and Major Deevers were able to report that the bridgehead was still intact. Two hours had passed since Sergeant Drabik had stepped onto the east bank of the Rhine and so far the German response had been minimal;

Our troops holding high ground on east side of river. Their positions receiving heavy 20mm and mortar fire from the west bank of the river [Victoriasberg Heights] *and 1,000 yards left of Remagen* [Unkel].

Prisoners file across the bridge into captivity. National Archives 111-SC-201874-S

German flak gun on the east bank of the Rhine were silenced by Captain Soumas' tanks. J William Mustanich/Friedensmuseum

Sketch of the crossing made by Sergeant Eugene Dorland of the 9th Armored Engineer Battalion.

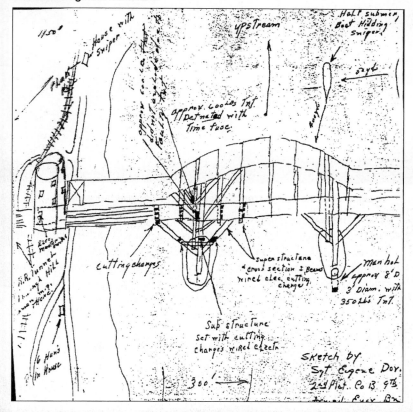

Looking over the bridge from Erpler Ley.   Stang/Friedensmuseum

The Missing Artillery Regiment

As 27th Armored Infantry Battalion began to establish itself on the east bank, Colonel Engeman was informed that a regiment of artillery was hidden in the woods to the west of the Victoriasberg Heights. It was the missing regiment of the 277th *Volksgrenadier* Division that Major Scheller had waited for earlier that morning. A prisoner of war believed that the two

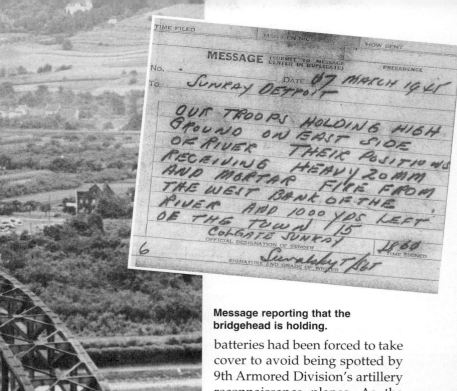

Message reporting that the bridgehead is holding.

batteries had been forced to take cover to avoid being spotted by 9th Armored Division's artillery reconnaissance planes. As the American CCB advanced, the guns had become cut off from Remagen. They had attempted to cut across country but the horse drawn carriages had bogged down. Engeman instructed Lieutenant Dmitri Paris, commander of his light tank company, to find the artillery regiment. His men eventually found twelve horse drawn guns in the woods south of Plattborn.

News begins to spread

While 27th Armored Infantry Battalion began to dig in on the far bank of the Rhine, Brigadier Hoge was still seeking assurance that he should continue to send men across the river. Having heard nothing from divisional headquarters, he decided to return to his command post to try and make contact. However, a short time after he arrived at Birresdorf, Major-General Leonard arrived. General Leonard later recalled discussion:

> *Early in the afternoon I had been down with CCA in what appeared to be the main drive to the south towards the Ahr River. I came up to the CCB command post at Birresdorf and General Hoge was there, having just returned from looking at the bridge from the high ground overlooking Remagen. General Hoge said 'Well we got the bridge', I said, That's a hell of a note. Now we got the bull by the tail, and caused a lot of trouble. But let's push it and then put it up to corps.*

Now he had the support of his superior officer, Brigadier Hoge was able to concentrate on sending all his troops across the river.

Although 27th Armored Infantry Battalion had managed to form roadblocks either side of the bridge and secured the high ground overlooking the crossing, the toehold could easily be driven into the river by a strong counterattack. Some were

The driver of a halftrack keeps watch for enemy aircraft from the streets of Remagen. National Archives 111-SC-202241

concerned the Germans might still have the means to blow up the bridge isolating Major Deevers' men on the far bank. Major-General Leonard outlined his own personal fears later; he wondered '... whether the sons of b-----s had put some delayed time-bombs on the bridge.' Even so he cancelled the order to push south to the River Ahr and encouraged Brigadier Hoge to support the crossing with all the available men and vehicles in the area. He considered that it was better to push men across and fight on although he '...still figured that it might be an enemy trap, but he concluded that it would be better to risk the sacrifice of having the force cut off by a blown bridge'.

After consultation with Brigadier-General Hoge the two agreed to probe the German defences at the first opportunity,

We did some scratching of our heads at first, but General Hoge and I agreed that we couldn't even think of coming back once we had pushed across. The only thing to do was to exploit the bridgehead.

Even if the bridge collapsed landing craft and DUKW's could ferry supplies across the river while engineers built temporary crossings.

While the two studied the problems caused by the unexpected crossing, Captain Robert W Alexander, Leonard's Aide, drove back to divisional headquarters in Stadt Meckenheim to report the news. Although he managed to contact III Corps, General Millikin was away at 78th Infantry Division's headquarters and Alexander asked for advice what to do about the unexpected turn in events. Colonel Harry Johnson, Millikin's Chief of Staff, was in no doubt what his commanding officer would want; cancel the offensive operation south of the Ahr River and exploit the Remagen bridgehead with every available man.

The first night
As darkness fell Major-General Leonard took steps to send troops to Remagen. 9th Armored Division's original plan to drive south across the Ahr River, meant that the bulk of the infantry was several hours away. Trucks were sent to Bad Godesberg to collect the 1/310th Infantry Regiment and transport the men to the bridge, while the 47th Infantry Regiment, the 52nd and the 60th Armored Infantry Battalions were also directed to move to Remagen at the earliest

opportunity. In the meantime Brigadier Hoge planned how to reinforce his men on the far bank. He was relieved to hear that the 52nd Armored Infantry Battalion had cleared the village of Kripp before nightfall, eliminating the chance of a German counterattack on the west bank. It was one less thing to worry about.

Meanwhile, the situation at the bridge was still causing him concerns, the infantry on the far bank desperately needed armoured support. Although Company A of the 14th Tank Battalion was waiting impatiently to cross, the engineers were still trying to make the bridge safe for vehicles. The damage caused by the explosion on the north pier had ripped out a large part of the timber decking. A brief survey had shown that the main structure had survived the blast more or less intact nevertheless, real damage to the girders was still a matter of some concern. The engineers still needed their supply of stout timber to effect repairs. As the hours passed, search parties failed to turn up anything useful and eventually Brigadier Hoge gave permission to remove timber from local properties.

As Major Deevers men waited anxiously for reinforcements, news that troops had managed to establish a crossing over the

The damaged decking reduced traffic across the bridge to single file.
National Archives 111-SC-202370-S

Armoured troops make their way towards Remagen. National Archives 111-SC-421363

Rhine was beginning to spread. As early as 19:30 the staff at the 52nd Armoured Infantry Battalion knew that they were soon to be on the move when a liaison officer arrived with news that all previous orders had been cancelled and Lieutenant-Colonel Price had been summoned to CCB Headquarters. Forty minutes later he returned and called a meeting with his company commanders to brief them on their new orders. In the meantime, drivers were ordered to warm up the vehicles and the men had to be ready to move out immediately.

An advance party set off at 20:30 to contact CCB Headquarters and make the necessary arrangements prior to the main force moving out an hour later. Little did the GIs know that they would spend most of the night on the road, snarled up in a huge traffic jam as vehicles carrying men and equipment tried to make their way into Remagen. It would take six hours to travel little over six miles; the 52nd Armored Infantry Battalion's experiences were typical on the roads leading to Remagen that night.

Tanks begin to cross the bridge

As reinforcements began to head towards Remagen, Brigadier Hoge was relieved to hear that the bridge was finally ready to accept vehicles. A queue of vehicles, including 27th Armored Infantry Battalion's abandoned halftracks were blocking many of the roads through the town and in an attempt to relieve the congestion. Hoge had ordered spare vehicles to park on the side roads, leaving Koblenzstrasse free for traffic heading for the bridge.

Hoge wanted his towed anti-tank guns to cross first but an unexpected delay meant that Captain Soumas' company of tanks went first. The dozer tank that had stood guard on the approach ramp was ordered to move out of the way and at 00:15 on 8 March the first Sherman tank edged its way tentatively onto the bridge. As the driver followed the white tape strung out to guide them forward, the rest of the crew watched anxiously. Captain Soumas later recalled how,

> They made the trip without incident, except that their passage over the planking was accompanied by an ominous and nerve-wracking creaking.

Over the next thirty minutes Engeman's nine Shermans crossed over the bridge and made their way down onto the river road. Following advice from the engineers Colonel Engeman decided

Infantry and tanks make their way onto the east bank of the Rhine. National Archives 111-SC-202358

to leave his four Pershing tanks on the Remagen side of the river. Although they were sorely needed on the east bank of the river, no one could be sure that the temporary repair would be able to support them.

Five tanks turned west heading down the Erpel road in search of Company A. However, before they established contact with the infantry, German engineers launched a counterattack in the hope of reaching the bridge with explosives. The tank crews fired blindly into the darkness with their 0.5 calibre machine guns as the Germans closed in and at one point, crew members had to throw grenades from the turret hatch to drive them off. Captain Soumas recalls how close the Germans came to reaching the bridge,

> Only a few minutes after the northern roadblock had been established, the enemy staged an infantry counterattack in its vicinity. It was too dark to tell from which direction the attack came; the roadblock was descended upon by swarms of Germans and a great deal of shooting resulted. The counterattack was beaten off, but no prisoners were taken because of the darkness. The next morning ten Germans came out of holes in the vicinity and surrendered.

The surviving German engineers withdrew to report to Major Bödicker that the road was strongly held. Little did they know how close they had come to achieving their objective.

The disappearance of the infantry puzzled many for some time, however, an interview with Major Russell, 27th Armored Infantry Battalion's Intelligence Officer, some weeks later may provide the answer. During the course of the night the men on the far bank were naturally on edge. Although the upper echelons were delighted to have established a foothold on the east bank of the Rhine, the GIs in the front line were concerned by the lack of armour and halftracks. Everyone realised that the Germans would counterattack at the first opportunity and noises heard in the distance soon started rumours amongst the men that tanks were on their way to attack them. As the night wore on men started to drift back towards the bridge and some began crossing the river.

> ... someone started a rumour that the troops on the east side were to withdraw. Major Russell states that unfortunately this rumour was started by an officer, which gave it a ring of truth. There was no excuse for the rumour having started and the only

apparent reason for it was a desire of this officer to get back where it was safe.

As a consequence, during the early hours of the 8th, about a third of 27th Armored Infantry Battalion returned to the Remagen side of the river, leaving the bridgehead extremely exposed. Fortunately, officers on the west bank soon detected the unauthorised withdrawal and within the hour the men had returned across the river.

While his men battled for survival on the Erpel road, Captain Soumas led his remaining tanks towards the town of Kasbach, joining Company C's roadblock 800 metres east of the bridge. Before long his crews faced a second attack by German engineers trying to reach the bridge. Under cover of darkness Major Strobel had assembled sixty men in Hönnigen. The plan was to carry explosives along the riverbank and slip past the roadblock undetected. A counterattack against the town of Orsberg was arranged to start at the same time in the hope of creating a diversion.

Leutnant Auch almost succeeded in getting his men past the tank roadblock, but they were detected as they closed in on the bridge. Fifteen were rounded up and taken prisoner in the

Looking over Erpel towards the Ludendorff Bridge.
National Archives 111-SC-202634

Major Herbert Strobel gathered sixty men and organised a counter attack.
Friedensmuseum

retreat that followed. A second attempt made a few hours later also ended in failure, resulting in another twenty-two of Strobel's men being captured.

The attack on Orsberg was also doomed to failure. A mixed group of German infantry and engineers made their way down the Bruchhausen road, not knowing what to expect. There had been no time to reconnoitre the American positions and as they stumbled on Company A's line of foxholes, the Germans came under heavy fire. In the confusion that followed, panic set in and the Germans withdrew towards Bruchhausen, thinking that Orsberg was strongly held.

As the Germans probed 27th Armored Infantry Battalion's perimeter, Company B on top of Erpeler Ley spent an uncomfortable night. It was reported:

At 01:00 an enemy artillery barrage of 23 rounds fell; all but three, however, were duds. Protection against artillery was meagre. The men could not dig foxholes in the stone. We just had to lie there and sweat it out.

Adolf Hitler Strasse in Remagen was renamed Yankstrasse. National Archives 111-SC-201957-S

Fortunately, the Germans decided against attacking the hill and Leutnant Liedike's men only encountered one German, an artillery observer, attempting to return to his post. As Major Deevers' infantry and the handful of tanks fought off attacks against the bridgehead, many of them were beginning to wonder where the promised reinforcements were.

The 52nd Armored Infantry Battalion had finally reached Remagen, having spent the past few hours stuck in traffic. The plan was to send the infantry across on foot along with the halftracks towing their anti-tank guns. At 02:00 Lieutenant-Colonel Prince's men left their halftracks and within the hour Company C began to file along the pedestrian walkway at the same time that a tank destroyer, the first of its type to cross the bridge, edged its way onto the decking.

Company C of the 656th Tank Destroyer Battalion had begun to arrive in Remagen shortly after midnight and as they lined up ready to cross, sporadic artillery fire targeted the town while German snipers trapped on the west bank fired into the darkness. At 03:00 Captain Tuggle, the Company CO, was finally given orders to cross and the column of tank destroyers moved up the approach ramp led by Sergeant Miller's jeep. Guides waved the column onto the bridge, making sure that they followed the white line painted on the decking. At first all went well but as Sergeant Jaroscak's tank destroyer crawled forward, disaster struck. Upon passing the second pier, the temporary timbers over the damaged decking slipped, sending the vehicle lurching forward. It finally came to rest on the bridge girders and despite Sergeant Jaroscak's attempts to free his tank destroyer, one track was unable to maintain a grip. The vehicle was stuck and nothing could pass.

For the next three hours the engineers and tank crews struggled to free the stricken tank, using crowbars and towropes

A military policeman studies the sign proudly erected by the 9th Armored Division. National Archives 111-SC-202242

to try and pull it back onto the decking. Meanwhile, Captain Soumas waited anxiously on the far bank to greet the tank destroyers and as the hours passed he sent numerous requests for news as to where they were. Finally, at 06:00 he discovered what the hold up was:

TD is stuck on bridge, trying to pull from this side, stand by
in case needed, if traffic starts flowing, not needed.

Although no vehicles could cross, the 52nd Armored Infantry

Having crossed the bridge, troops make their way down to the river road.
National Archives 111-SC-202357

Battalion continued to file past the bottleneck on foot and by 04:00 all three companies were on the far bank. Lieutenant-Colonel Prince was ordered to take over the west side of the bridgehead, covering Erpel and part of 27th Armored Infantry Battalion's perimeter around Orsberg and by first light the battalion was in place, ready to face any counterattacks from the direction of Unkel or Bruchhausen.

1/310th Infantry Regiment had begun to arrive at midnight and as the GIs assembled in the centre of the town they were confronted by a mass of lorries and halftracks. Military police herded the battalion through the packed streets down to the bridge and at 04:00 the first men of the battalion stepped on the east side of the Rhine. Having secured the western half of the bridgehead, Brigadier Hoge now wanted to expand the eastern side towards Kasbach. In the meantime 2nd Platoon scaled Eperler Ley to head across country towards the village, the rest of the company made their way along he river road. They had only marched 150 metres when the head of the column stumbled on a German patrol that had managed to slip past the roadblock. Seven men were taken prisoner and a quick search showed that they were carrying explosives obviously intended for the bridge. After sending the prisoners to the rear, Company B moved into Kasbach, finding the small cluster of houses and factory deserted and by first light the 1/310th Infantry Regiment was holding a perimeter on the high ground around Ockenfels.

Although Brigadier Hoge's plan to deny the Germans of the high ground around the bridge was beginning to take shape, the lack of armour and anti-tank guns was extremely worrying.

The American engineers finally freed the trapped tank destroyer at 06:00, after three hours of backbreaking work and once more the column of vehicles began to move. They were just in time. With dawn approaching Brigadier Hoge was concerned that his men would soon be facing more counterattacks. His infantry would stand little chance of survival if the Germans had managed to bring tanks into the area during the night. At first light Hoge ordered all his subordinate commanders to cross over to the east bank and set up their command posts close to their units. There was still a chance that a lucky artillery shell could bring the bridge down and if it did, he intended to fight on in the hope that ferries and amphibious vehicles could keep him supplied until engineers could build temporary bridges.

Work starts on temporary crossings across the Rhine

As troops began to pour into Remagen, General Millikin's main concern was how to increase the flow of traffic across the river. The Ludendorff Bridge was reduced to one-way only and no one expected it to be able to supply more than a few hundred men. As columns of trucks and halftracks made their way to the bridge through the dark night, filling roads for miles around Remagen, plans were being made to provide alternative crossings. Colonel F R Lyons, III Corps' chief engineer was familiar with the Remagen area, having served with the Army of Occupation as the local commander in 1918.

It would take several days to install pontoon bridges across the Rhine and in the meantime Lyons planned to establish a series of ferries north and south of the bridge. Naval Unit No 1, equipped with twenty-four LCVP (Landing Craft Vehicle, Personnel), was ordered to start a ferry service within hours of the initial crossing. Each LCVP was capable of carrying either twenty-four men, four tons of supplies or a vehicle up to three quarters of a ton in weight. They could be put into operation almost immediately, operating a shuttle service across the river.

However, III Corps also needed to send tanks, anti-tank guns and heavy equipment across the Rhine and General Millikin had directed 86th Engineer Heavy Pontoon Battalion to the Remagen area with orders to start building rafts capable of carrying tanks. Millikin wanted three ferries, one adjacent to the bridge, the second to the north and the third to the south, to relieve the traffic situation around Remagen. It also meant that each part of the bridgehead could operate independently if the

Infantry climb aboard an LCVP to make the crossing. National Archives 111-SC-203132

Tanks were floated across the river on makeshift pontoons. National Archives 111-SC-222569

Landing craft ferried troops and equipment across the Rhine until temporary bridges were built. National Archives 111-SC-335580

A DUKW ferries troops across the Rhine to Erpel. National Archives 111-SC-203131.

Germans managed to break through to the riverbank at any point.

The American engineers managed to reach their respective crossing points on 8 March and began to build their temporary rafts. Pontoons were floated into the river and strapped together before covering the assembly with timber decking; a twenty-two horsepower outboard motor would power the ferry across the Rhine.

Throughout the day landing craft and pontoons ferried troops and equipment across the river and although they managed to supplement the traffic crossing the bridge, new crossings would have to be built to sustain the bridgehead on the far bank

CHAPTER EIGHT

ESTABLISHING THE BRIDGEHEAD

At first light on 8 March Brigadier Hoge reviewed his situation and began to plan how to expand the bridgehead. Although men were pouring into the Remagen area, Hoge needed space to deploy them on the east bank of the river. The rugged terrain compounded the congested nature of the bridgehead and there would be few opportunities to deploy regiments as a whole. In fact Hoge would be forced to split up the battalions, deploying them as and how he saw fit. It would make communication and cooperation difficult as the battalion commanders found themselves operating under new makeshift commands.

One immediate priority was to continue clearing the hills overlooking Remagen to deny the Germans direct observation of the bridge. Although 27th Armored Infantry Battalion had

Infantry of the 78th Division are carried through the streets of Remagen.
National Archives 111-SC-421362

already secured Orsberg, they only held the rim of the high ground overlooking the river. Brigadier Hoge was concerned that a German counterattack from Bruchhausen could drive the battalion off the heights, bringing the enemy within striking distance of the bridge. Consequently, Hoge planned to send the 2nd Battalion of the 47th Infantry Regiment up to Orsberg, with orders to attack Bruchhausen. The Regiment's 1st Battalion would also head up the hill to Orsberg before swinging north to descend into Scheuren and Rheinbreitbach. It was hoped that the two battalions would be able to secure the northeast sector of the bridgehead.

Once 47th Infantry Regiment had secured its objective, the 311th Infantry Regiment, which was expected to cross before

midday, could advance north along the riverbank. The leading battalion would take Honnef and the high ground surrounding the town, while the second in line swung east to secure Himberg; the remaining battalion would fill the gap between the two.

Meanwhile, the terrain south of the bridge posed a serious problem to Brigadier Hoge's plans. The only road south ran along the riverbank and for most of its length it was overlooked by steep wooded hills crowned by villages. The only way to advance east was via steep narrow roads that wound their way up ravines to the crests of hills. The tanks and infantry would have to work in close cooperation to avoid being ambushed. At first light Brigadier Hoge planned to send the third battalion of

the 47th Infantry Regiment to seize Ohlenberg, one of the villages overlooking the river road. It would block the road from Kalenborn, the most likely route for a German counterattack. Meanwhile, the 1st Battalion of the 310th Infantry Regiment would push east from Kasbach to clear Ockenfels while the 60th Armored Infantry Battalion pushed south along the road past Linz and Dattenberg.

Brigadier Hoge's plan was to create a wide bridgehead, five miles north and three miles south of the bridge, as early as possible. Meanwhile, he would aim to push east at a steady rate through the Westerwald, keeping the Germans on the move to deny them the opportunity to dig in. It was an ambitious plan and it relied on the steady flow of reinforcements

Brigadier Hoge's first priority was to clear the hills overlooking the bridge.

95

Traffic congestion on the west bank of the river severely limited the flow of troops across the bridge. National Archives 111-SC-203733

across the bridge. In a later interview Hoge lamented how the congestion on the west bank would let the opportunity for exploitation slip away;

> *It did not work as fast as we had expected; we had twelve battalions on paper, and had they arrived on schedule, we could have walked through the opposition, but the enemy had a little time to get set.*

During the morning Major-General Leonard crossed the Ludendorff Bridge to review the plan. He left content that his subordinate was fully in control of the bridgehead; all that was needed now was reinforcements.

Holding Erpel

The third platoon of C Company 656th Tank Destroyer Battalion was directed north along the river road past Erpel, where it joined 52nd Infantry Battalion's roadblock covering the approach from Unkel. Although there were no signs of activity along the road, Lieutenant Lowry's men noticed a river barge sailing up the river from the direction of Honnef. With a mixture of curiosity and suspicion they watched as it drew closer. Of the incident it is recorded,

> *They were just sitting there, blocking the road, when around the bend in the river came a boat. They did not know if it was an Allied engineer's boat or what. Through glasses Lt Lowry could see someone in a German uniform. He called to the first tank destroyer*

German POWs carry wounded GIs to safety. National Archives/Friedensmuseum

to open fire on it. There were trees in front so the first TD could not fire. Sergeant Batdorf's destroyer with Corporal Miller as gunner could see the boat and fired a round at it. The shot hit but went high. APC ammunition was used and it exploded on the other side of the boat. The personnel on the boat whipped out a white flag. The boat was a long boat shaped like a tug. It had another boat or barge, which it was pulling with it. The gunner lowered his sight

Keeping watch for saboteurs along the river. National Archives 111-SC-360968

An endless column of men and vehicles crossed the bridge around the clock. National Archives 111-SC-203736

and shot. The shell hit the water line. The third shot hit home and the Germans raised everything they had that was white.

Ten soldiers were eventually rescued from the two boats and after cross-examination Lieutenant Lowry discovered that they had sailed up river from Cologne, over ten miles, hoping to be taken prisoner.

47th Infantry Regiment advances into Bruchhausen

The 2/47th Infantry Regiment had reached Remagen at 04:00 and managed to cross the river before first light. Brigadier Hoge immediately sent it up the heights to Orsberg to join the 27th Armored Infantry Battalion's outposts on the ridge. Brigadier Hoge had tanks available, but they were unable to climb the steep gradient to reach the village. The 2/47th would have to advance unsupported. Cautiously moving northeast across the open fields, the lead company came under small arms fire as it approached the village of Bruchhausen. Pushing on, the battalion managed to enter the streets, driving a small German rearguard before them. By late afternoon it had managed to clear the village but as the GIs began to dig in along the eastern outskirts three Panzer IVs and a number of halftracks emerged from the woods to the east.

Mainstay of the German armoured divisions, the *Panzerkampfwagen* Mk IV.

As the German infantry began to dismount the 2/47th opened fire with every available weapon while calling in close artillery support. It appeared that the Germans were not expecting to find Bruchhausen occupied and before long they withdrew into the woods to regroup. It had been a close call. If the 2/47th had arrived any later the German armour would have been able to attack Orsberg, less than half a mile from the bridge.

As the 2/47th fought for Bruchhausen, the 1st Battalion had moved up to Orsberg, turning north towards Scheuren. As the GIs descended into the valley they came under fire, but once again there were only a few Germans outposting the village. A counterattack by fifty enemy infantry during the evening was easily repulsed and by nightfall the two battalions of the 47th Infantry Regiment had managed to establish a continuous

47th Infantry Regiment's defence of Bruchhausen.

Reconaissance troops make their way through Remagen. The sign warns of the severe consequences of listening to rumours. National Archives 111-SC-202343

defensive line. It meant that, for the time being, the Orsberg heights were safe. However, the next phase of Brigadier Hoge's plan, the advance along the river bank, had been frustrated by the late arrival of the 311th Infantry Regiment.

310th Infantry Regiment secures Linz

The 1st Battalion of the 310th Infantry Regiment had crossed the river before first light and occupied Kasbach. The plan was for Company C and four tanks of the 14th Tank Battalion to advance along the river road towards Linz, working in cooperation with the 1st Battalion of the 310th Infantry Regiment. They set off at 09:00, with the infantry covering the road and searching for mines. It appeared that the Germans had fled and the only contact with the enemy was with four German soldiers trying to escape in an American jeep. The orderly and his three startled passengers, a major and two *leutnants*, were taken prisoner and sent to the rear. As the column moved slowly forward alongside the river, a second jeep was seen coming up the road from the direction of Linz. This time the occupants were wearing US Army uniforms. It was Captain Gibble, 27th

100

Armoured Infantry Battalion's chaplain and he had welcome news:

> As they approached the town they were informed that it had surrendered and had been declared an open town because there was a large hospital full of enemy wounded there. This information came from Captain William T Gibble, a Chaplain to whom the town had surrendered. Chaplain Gibble told Captain Soumas that LINZ was free of snipers and all enemy except wounded and medical personnel.

Brigadier Hoge was delighted to hear the news, it meant that he could expand his bridgehead a considerable distance without a fight. If the Germans had decided to defend Linz and the neighbouring hill, the Kaiserberg, they would have been in a suitable position to block the river road. Instead, Soumas' tanks followed the infantry through the town unopposed and formed a roadblock facing Dattenberg. Meanwhile, 1st Battalion's Company A followed close behind, heading north up the hill to occupy Ockenfels. So far it appeared as though the plan to expand the southern half of the bridgehead was progressing well.

While Captain Soumas' men congratulated themselves on their good luck, the peace was suddenly shattered when they came under fire. As the tank crews scrambled for cover and began to look for the threat, they discovered that they were in a dangerous situation.

> The tanks had been in position about an hour when they drew bazooka and small arms fire, evidently from inside the town. This came as a surprise, in view of what Chaplain Gibble had said, but Soumas decided to prepare his force for an enemy counterattack. In assembling what infantry he had, he discovered that there were no more than fifteen men available.

Fearing that his tanks could be overrun, Captain Soumas contacted CCB's headquarters for assistance: '...down in town Linz, no doughs around, bazooka men are around my tanks, have to withdraw to edge of town.'

Brigadier Hoge responded by recalling the infantry company from Ockenfels and once they had retraced their steps down the hill, Lieutenant Durham's men joined Captain Soumas. After securing the roadblock, a platoon of infantry and two tanks headed through the town in search of the snipers. Once on the outskirts of the town they took up positions covering the

A military policeman waits to guide reinforcements along the Erpel road.
National Archives 111-SC-334096

Kalenborn road. It appeared that there were no Germans in the area, but as Captain Soumas climbed out of his tank to brief the men, a sniper opened fire from a nearby church tower. Luckily no one was hurt and two squads went in search of the sniper, returning before nightfall with five prisoners. Linz had been secured and as more reinforcements crossed the river, Brigadier Hoge could look forward to securing Dattenberg and the last hill overlooking the bridge.

311th Infantry Regiment's attack on Unkel

The congestion on the west bank had delayed 311th Infantry Regiment by several hours and leaving Neukirchen, Colonel Chester Willingham was frustrated by the amount of traffic on the roads. The infantry were desperately needed to reinforce the bridgehead, yet they spent most of the day waiting in the backs of trucks. The hold up was frustrating Brigadier Hoge's plan for a rapid advance towards Honnef, and as the hours passed, he was aware that the Germans could be assembling in Unkel, preparing to counterattack.

The 1st Battalion, led by Lieutenant-Colonel Lyle Kennedy, eventually reached Remagen during the afternoon and while it waited to cross the river it appeared that every German artillery piece in the area was targeting the bridge. Lorries queued up for their turn to run the gauntlet of shrapnel. The military police waited for pauses in the shelling before ordering them to cross.

While the 1st Battalion assembled in Erpel the 3rd Battalion,

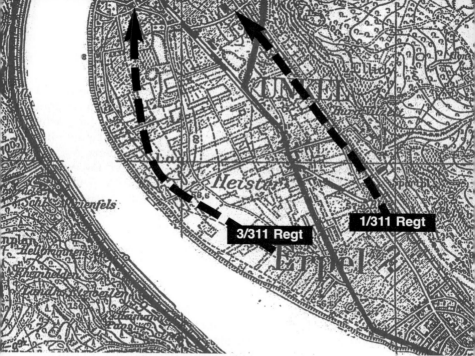

led by Lieutenant-Colonel Andy Lipscomb, crossed the river. It was late afternoon by the time Colonel Willingham's men were ready to move out. The 1st Battalion advanced alongside the railway line towards Heister while 3rd Battalion made its way tentatively along the riverbank. Hoge's fears were realised as the infantry came under heavy small arms fire as they approached the outskirts of the village.

Nine Shermans from 14th Tank Battalion's Company C provided covering fire as the two battalions edged closer to Unkel but they had little effect on the German positions. A message to 14th Tank Battalion's commanding officer sums up

Armoured troops on the move. National Archives 111-SC-336901

the situation, 'Doughs say they need more big boys – If I can't have any, what do I do with what I have?'

In the face of determined resistance 1st Battalion managed to secure Heister before nightfall and, after bypassing the centre of Unkel, it closed in on Scheuren. There was no sign of any white flags and Lieutenant-Colonel Kennedy expected to have to fight for the village. He did not have to wait long. 20mm AA guns opened fire as soon as the infantry advanced towards the outskirts, drawing fire from the Sherman tanks. So far there had been no answer to the plea for extra armour and 1st Battalion had to push with the few tanks it had. After several hours the Germans eventually withdrew and as darkness fell Lieutenant-Colonel Kennedy's men were able to begin a house-to-house search.

The light was beginning to fade by the time 311th Infantry Regiment's 2nd Battalion reached the east bank of the Rhine. As the GIs assembled in Erpel few would have been aware that they belonged to the first complete regiment to cross the river. Now that Brigadier Hoge had adequate forces in the northern part of the bridgehead, he was determined to attack the village of Unkel at the first opportunity. Under cover of darkness the 3rd Battalion advanced with a platoon of Tank Destroyers in support, but before long the leading company came under heavy machine gun fire. A German strongpoint covered the approaches to the village was blocking the way forward. Lieutenant-Colonel Lipscomb called up the tank destroyers in the hope of reviving the advance.

They [the infantry] left it up to Lt Lowery how to do it. Both APC and HE were used. The ready rack was fired at a range of about fifteen feet. The flash of the gun completely blinded the entire crew. The destroyer was returned to cover and another destroyer was backed into firing position and fired while the first destroyer loaded its ready rack. Lt Lowery told his crew to keep their eyes closed and to stay covered up while the others fired so that when they went forward, they could see. The third destroyer was used to spray the buildings with .05 calibre machine gun fire. They were getting direct machine gun fire on the turret of their destroyers. Ten of the enemy were trying to escape. Five were killed by intentional enemy fire. The German officer in charge ordered the men to stay at the guns and when they ran they were fired on.

Once the threat had been removed the infantry were able to move forward into the outskirts of Unkel. They advanced cautiously searching every house en route but despite the presence of armour, the Germans put up a stiff fight, pouring fire indiscriminately into the darkness. In the confusion, reports of heavy casualties along the main street began to worry Lieutenant-Colonel Lipscomb. It appeared that the Germans were holding a series of fortified houses which the infantry were unable to outflank. Once again Lipscomb called up the tank destroyers to deal with the threat. 2nd Platoon's After-Action Report illustrates the vicious nature of the fighting in Unkel;

> *He* [Sergeant Miller] *reported to a Captain who gave him the situation and told him that the task force was to be moved down the street, but the street was covered by eight machine guns which had accounted for about fifty infantrymen. The TD men couldn't see the men and didn't know how it* [the situation] *ran. Sergeant Miller pulled up two destroyers and fired down the street. Houses were set on fire by these shots. They fired at the first four houses with APC. He was told not to fire HE because of the wounded men in the street. Enemy returned fire and never took cover. The tracer fire was coming up, so we figured they were in the cellars. Once again Sergeant Miller asked permission to fire HE but didn't get it because of the wounded men in the street. All the while they were firing 76mm, they were also firing the .50 calibre machine guns, spraying all the houses but keeping it away from the wounded men. They fired more APC and .05 calibre but still got returning fire. They then used white phosphorous hand grenades to get more light. It was a pitch dark night. When the grenades went off, they could see most of the way down the street.*

German prisoners are escorted through the outskirts of Remagen. National Archives 111-SC-202240

They saw no wounded men in the street so took a chance and fired HE into the houses. At that time both 76mm guns jammed. Cause is unknown. Pulled back again and reported to the Infantry captain telling him that the streets were clear for 150 yards and that no casualties were received. Twenty-four rounds of 76mm ammunition and 2,000 rounds of .05 calibre were expended.

Tanks and tank destroyers continued to work closely with the infantry and after a night of fierce fighting, Colonel Willingham was able to report that Unkel was clear. Over two hundred prisoners had been taken in the battle anddozens more had been killed.

The attack on Ohlenberg

Having secured the river road as far south as Linz, Brigadier Hoge turned his attentions towards Ohlenberg on the heights overlooking the river. It was less than half a mile from the river and the Germans would be able to use the road from Kalenborn to launch a counterattack towards Kasbach, the shortest route to the bridge.

Brigadier Hoge ordered the 3rd Battalion of the 47th Infantry Regiment to secure the village as soon as it had crossed the Rhine and at 19:30 the battalion began to climb the heights heading for the village. As the infantry advanced cautiously up the wooded slopes towards their objective they came under heavy fire; German infantry, supported by armour were waiting for them. The after-action report sums up the bitter fighting for Ohlenberg,

This attack brought out some of the most stubborn resistance encountered in the REMAGEN bridgehead. The advance was made under heavy small arms fire, self-propelled gun and tank fire, and the town itself consisted of a series of strong points. Enemy infantry had to be cleaned out house by house. Direct tank and self-propelled gun fire from the North and East sections made this task a difficult one.

The battle raged on throughout the night but eventually the Germans withdrew northeast along the Kalenborn road to regroup. Brigadier Hoge was pleased to hear that the threat had been removed, but there was little respite for the men of the 47th Infantry Regiment. As they dug in on the northern outskirts of Ohlenberg, artillery targeted their shallow foxholes as the Germans prepared to counterattack.

The Plan for 9 March

At 02:00 on 9 March, Major-General Louis Craig, of the 9th Infantry Division, took over command of operations on the east bank of the Rhine from Brigadier Hoge. The base of the Remagen bridgehead was now three miles wide, stretching from Unkel in the north to Linz in the south, however, in places it was still less than a mile deep and a determined counterattack could force the Americans back to the river. The main areas of concern were the roads leading through the wooded hills to Bruchhausen and Ohlenberg. Aerial reconnaissance revealed that German armour was indeed heading towards the bridgehead and at high speed:

> Second TAC Air Force reports tonight that about 22:30 large columns of vehicles coming from northeast and south apparently heading in our direction. Columns using lights. Targets coming from northeast estimated about 25 minutes out. British working over them. So are our night fighters' ceiling too low to do much good. All units must be on alert for vehicles or any other signs of activity.

General Millikin wanted the bridgehead to be expanded to a width of five miles along the river. This would allow his engineers to build new bridges out of the range of mortars and

The crew of an anti-aircraft gun keep watch over the bridge. National Archives 111-SC-361071

machine guns. He also wanted Craig to push east to a depth of two miles, clearing the Germans from the high ground immediately overlooking the river. He could then carry out the second stage of his plan, advancing east to cut the road running through Kretzhaus, four miles northeast of Remagen. In doing so he would deny the Germans freedom of movement to deploy their armour.

311th Infantry Regiment's advance to Honnef

After fighting through the night for Unkel, the 311th Infantry Regiment was given little time to rest. General Craig was anxious to expand the bridgehead north, clearing Honnef before the Germans could occupy the town in force. The 1st Battalion was given the task of entering the town from the south and it advanced along the riverbank with three companies abreast. At first the battalion made good progress, however as soon as it reached the outskirts of the Honnef it became clear that the Germans intended to fight for the town,

> ... *enemy resistance in this city was stiffer than was expected and as the Battalion entered the town the enemy withdrew in a house to house retreat. It was noted that as the enemy withdrew he did not fight from every house as he had done on the west bank of the Rhine. Instead only the most strategically located houses were defended.*

With the aid of tanks and tank destroyers, 1st Battalion cleared

Panzerkampfwagen Mk V, better known as the Panther.

street after street and by nightfall it had managed to reach the centre of Honnef.

Meanwhile, the 3rd Battalion had managed to clear out the last elements of resistance in Unkel. Five Shermans of the 14th Tank Battalion gave close support to the infantry, successfully engaging a Panther tank while the GIs kept Germans armed with *panzerfausts* at bay. However, as the Battalion

311th Regiment's advance on Honnef.

German infantryman with a *panzerfaust*, a simple yet successful anti-tank weapon

completed its first objective one *panzerfaust* found its target, disabling Sergeant Herder's tank and wounding three crewmembers. It was a sharp reminder that tanks were extremely vulnerable in built up areas.

After clearing Scheuren, the battalion encountered stiff resistance as they entered Rheinbreitbach to the north. The After-Action report succinctly notes that 'the Germans elected to fight for every room of every house'. A Panther tank was quickly knocked out, hit by a HE round followed by four armour-piercing rounds in quick succession. As the house clearing operation continued, Colonel Willingham ordered the 2nd Battalion forward to help but by the time it had deployed southeast of the village the Germans had withdrawn.

General Craig commended the 311th for its actions on 9 March, for it had secured the northern part of the bridgehead. As the Regiment dug in for the night and counted their losses, over seventy killed and wounded, 381 prisoners were making their way into captivity.

The heights east of Bruchhausen

While 311th Infantry Regiment pushed north towards Honnef, Colonel George W Smythe planned to advance towards the wooded hills overlooking Bruchhausen with two battalions of the 47th Infantry Regiment (the third battalion was in the southern half of the bridgehead). At 05:00 2nd Battalion moved out under cover of darkness towards Eischeider Kopf, the highest peak in the area. However, before Company G had moved far across the open fields, they were spotted. Enemy tanks and self-propelled guns opened fire from hidden positions, pinning the company down. It was obvious to Smythe that the Germans held strong positions in the woods and to avoid further casualties, he recalled his men to their start line. Meanwhile, the 1st Battalion managed to advance a short distance east of Bruchhausen before infantry opened fire from the woods ahead. Many fell back leaving Company B isolated astride the Kalenborn road. It was eventually forced to retire as the Germans closed in on its front and flanks.

By midday the two battalions were back in their foxholes, north and east of Bruchhausen. The Germans were able to take advantage of woods and high ground, leaving Colonel Smythe with few opportunities for exploitation.

Securing the St Severinsberg valley

52nd Armoured Infantry Battalion had spent the night billeted in Erpel but at 11:00am Lieutenant-Colonel Prince returned from Divisional headquarters with orders to move out at once. Intelligence suggested that the Germans might counterattack down the St Severinsberg valley to try and reach the bridge. The battalion was to counter the threat as soon as possible. The Battalion Journal outlines Prince's plans:

> CO gives orders to Company COs to move to Kasbach and be prepared to counterattack. Check all weapons and ammo, notify men when ready to move.
>
> Order of March: A, C, B, HQ, CP will be in Kasbach. Coy C

Troops continue to pour onto the east bank of the Rhine.
National Archives 111-SC-203734

GIs check their weapons before into action. National Archives 111-SC-360973

will go in on left of the road, north of the town, Coy A on right of road and Coy B at the road junction.

The Battalion moved out at 13:00 hours and before long it had established a series of defensive posts north of Kasbach ready to meet an attack. Patrols from the 89th Reconnaissance Squadron had already scouted past St Severinsberg that the road ended abruptly. While the GIs dug in, patrols from Company C searched the woods for signs of German troops. They returned empty handed. It appeared that the infantry had withdrawn onto the high ground. Although the Germans refrained from attacking, Lieutenant-Colonel Prince's positions were targeted by random artillery bombardments throughout the afternoon.

While officers looked for a suitable building for their headquarters they stumbled on a huge cache of German supplies stored in a warehouse in Kasbach. It was a further sign that the enemy had fled into the hills to reorganise and await reinforcements. 52nd Armoured Infantry Battalion's news meant that another sector of the bridgehead had been sealed off.

The Battle for Ohlenberg

While two of 47th Infantry Regiment's battalions were struggling to make progress at Bruchhausen, the 3rd Battalion had had a degree of success to the south. Throughout the night the battalion had engaged armour and infantry in Ohlenberg and by first light had managed to secure most of the village. Despite the long night of fighting, and the fact that snipers were still operating in the village, the battalion's work was far from complete.

> The 3rd Battalion attacked at 05:45 hours to seize the road in vicinity of 685217 [northeast of Ohlenberg] and immediately encountered fierce resistance. Company K succeeded in reaching the objective and at 16:45, Company L was moved up to reinforce them. Fire from enemy tanks, self propelled guns and small arms was extremely heavy on this position throughout the period and the Battalion suffered high casualties in maintaining it. The day's advances were made against a determined enemy amply supported by artillery, tanks and self-propelled guns and positions gained were subjected to numerous small counterattacks.

Although 3/47th Infantry Regiment had, to some degree, secured the Ohlenberg ridge, twenty-four hours of continuous fighting had taken its toll. Heavy casualties and fatigue had left the Battalion in an extremely vulnerable position, astride the most likely avenue for a German attack. As the troops spent the night digging in they could hear the ominous sounds of enemy armour gathering to the east.

Holding Linz to the south

While troops tried to secure a footing on the high ground, south east of the bridge, the 1/310th Infantry Regiment held on to its positions around Linz. For the present time it appeared as though the Germans were concentrating their efforts against other sectors of the bridgehead. The first signs of enemy activity came during the early hours of the following morning when Captain Soumas was alerted by the sounds of a tracked vehicle approaching from the direction of Ronigerhof. As the infantry took up positions around the roadblock, Soumas instructed them to hold their fire until the last minute fearing that they

Work on the Erpel bridge progressed in spite of heavy shelling. National Archives 111-SC-203735

Keeping watch for German aircraft. National Archives 111-SC-361072

might give his position away to the German halftrack coming up the road. Minutes passed as the halftrack crawled forward looking for signs of the roadblock:

> It did not stop until it was almost on top of the outposts of the roadblock. One of its crew was taken prisoner. The prisoner said that a counterattack was planned, and that the halftrack had been sent down the road to draw fire. The enemy knew that there were two American tanks in the vicinity, and was hoping that the approaching halftrack would induce them to fire and give away their position.

Captain Soumas' refusal to open fire had saved his men from a night attack.

Later that night Soumas was pleased to greet Lieutenant Magura's platoon of tanks from B Company. With extra tanks to hand he decided move the second roadblock towards Dattenberg but as the tanks headed south along the river road, disaster struck in the darkness:

> In moving out, they drew small arms fire, and one of them [a tank] ran over a mine, believed to be one of our own. The supposition was that the mine had been laid by another unit without their knowledge. Although the mine did no appreciable damage, the plan to move the block that night was abandoned.

Work starts on the treadway bridge

Lieutenant-Colonel David E Peregrin, 291st Combat Engineer Battalion's commanding officer, had initially estimated that it would take twenty-four hours to construct the crossing to Erpel. Although the engineers had been ready to start work on 8 March, the 988th Engineer Treadway Bridging Company did not reach Remagen until the following morning, having been held up in traffic for thirty-six hours. The unit diary gives a brief insight into what the engineers faced:

> Preparations for construction of a bridge across the Rhine River and initiation of construction under intense artillery fire, bombing and strafing attacks commenced at 09:30 on 9 March. The bridge received one direct hit and suffered damage through near misses.

Despite the shelling, which damaged cranes, trucks and air compressors, the engineers continued to work and the bridge began to grow at a rate of fifteen metres an hour. However, during the afternoon work came to an abrupt halt when a direct hit on the bridge destroyed fifteen floats and damaged many others. Although the repair work took six hours to complete by midnight the engineers had built over 400 feet of the treadway.

Bombing the Bridge

Following disastrous attempts to bomb the bridge with Stukas on 8 March (eight out of ten had been shot down), the Luftwaffe changed its tactics the following day. Six fighter planes, including Me109s, Me210s, FW190s and jet propelled Me262s flew low over the valley, in the hope of achieving a lucky strike. 413 Automatic Anti-Aircraft Battery was directly in the flight path of the planes and the gun crews noted that the

> tactics used by the planes differed from what was observed yesterday. The planes took more evasive action and in general, manoeuvred more prior to the bombing runs and flew at lower altitudes.

The fast moving planes were difficult targets, however, four planes were shot down and a fifth was damaged. D Battery's 'highlight' of the day came at 14:40 when a Me210 made its bombing run over Kripp. 'Gun Control', a new innovation, allowed a weapon to track a plane remotely by radar firing automatically at the optimum moment. One gun fired at the plane with a single round of M43A3 time fuse; as the shell hit home the Me210 burst into flame, crashing to the ground nearby. Once again the Luftwaffe had failed to destroy the Ludendorff Bridge.

The Messerschmitt Me 210 fighter bomber. The type was used to attack the bridge and one was brought down by a single artillery shell.

CHAPTER NINE

EXPANDING THE BRIDGEHEAD

Hitler was furious that the Americans had managed to establish a foothold on the east bank of the Rhine, robbing his Armies of the chance to regroup. On 8 March he had recalled *Generalfeldmarschall* Albert Kesselring, Commander in Chief South (OB SUD) from the Italian front and the following day he replaced *Feldmarschall* von Rundstedt as Commander in Chief of the West. Kesselring's orders were simple: eliminate the Remagen bridgehead as soon as possible. Every available infantry and artillery unit was being directed into the Westerwald and the 11th Panzer Division was already approaching the American salient as Kesselring took over his new command.

By first light on 10 March, General Craig's concerns about the speed the bridgehead was expanding were increasing. Although great advances had been made along the riverbank towards Honnef, it appeared that German resistance was stiffening.

Civilians look on as tanks make their way towards Remagen. National Archives 111-SC-202535

Meanwhile, the wooded hills to the northeast and east of the bridge presented few opportunities for exploitation and there concerns that the Germans were preparing to counterattack along the Ohlenberg ridge. Until the high ground overlooking Kretzhaus had been secured, General Craig would be unable to develop the southern tip of the bridgehead. As reinforcements queued up to take their turn to cross the river, the slow expansion of the bridgehead left little room to deploy them. General Craig was finding out for himself why General Bradley's planners had wanted to avoid crossing the Rhine opposite the difficult terrain of the Westerwald.

The 11th Panzer Division counterattacks Honnef
Although 311th Infantry Regiment had managed to secure the southern half of Honnef, General Craig wanted Colonel Willingham to complete the capture of the town to prevent German forces using it as a base to stage counterattacks. At 08:30 the 1st Battalion renewed house-clearing operations, but once again Lieutenant-Colonel Kennedy's men found that the

Honnef witnessed bitter street fighting; tanks engage a strongpoint while medics evacuate a wounded GI. National Archives

Germans were determined to hold onto every inch of ground.

The enemy continued to put up a stiff resistance in all sectors. There were no signs of enemy disorganisation or disorder. Every house was fought for and every defence was strongly fortified against our attacks. Enemy fortified positions in the form of metal doors in the enemy held houses, required demolition charges to crack them open.

Fighting continued throughout the day and although Kennedy's men were making slow progress, during the evening Company C encountered two Tiger tanks. They were the first signs that the 11th Panzer Division had begun to arrive. Although tanks and tank destroyers eventually helped to restore the company's positions, it was a worrying development. The question was, could Colonel Willingham's Regiment hold onto the town while fresh reinforcements were brought across the river.

While the 1st Battalion struggled to make headway in Honnef, the 3rd Battalion moved across country to the east to extend the Regiments' grip on the town. For once, the advance was virtually unopposed and by nightfall, Lieutenant-Colonel Lipscomb's companies were digging in beyond Mezenberg.

Throughout the 10 March the 1st and 2nd Battalions of the 47th Infantry Regiment maintained a defensive position north and east of Bruchhausen. The experience of the previous day had shown General Craig that there was little to gain from advancing in this sector while the Germans could send reinforcements from the Kalenborn area.

The German counterattack at Ohlenberg
The 2nd Battalion of 310th Infantry Regiment had left Heimersheim just after midnight en route for Remagen. The crossing was delayed for a time while engineers struggled to extricate a jeep which had become wedged in a gap in the timber decking. As the GIs waited to cross they watched while shells pounded the area around the bridge, occasionally the boredom was broken when shrapnel hit the steel girders, sending showers of sparks into the night sky. As dawn approached, Colonel Heyes eventually received the all clear from the military police to send his men over the bridge.

They headed east through Kasbach towards Ohlenberg to reinforce the 3rd Battalion of the 47th Infantry Regiment.

German armour stumbled on 2/310th Regiment as it assembled in Ohlenberg. National Archives 111-SC-335253

The Battle for Ohlenberg, showing the German breakthrough.

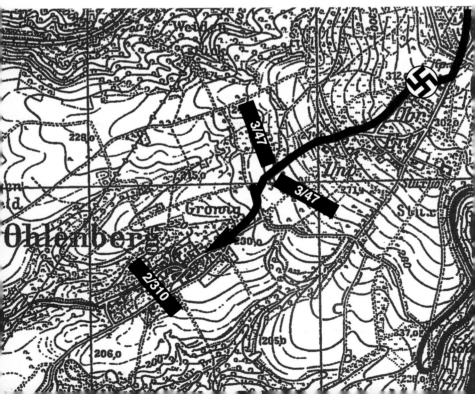

Although the battalion reached the village in good time as Colonel Heyes briefed his company commanders, the peace was shattered. As the battalion climbed the slopes towards Ohlenberg, a German counterattack had struck the 3/47th Infantry Regiment. Further, as Heyes men assembled, enemy halftracks and infantry suddenly appeared in the midst of their position. There was no time to organise, the battalion would have to fight were they stood. Men scattered to find cover in hedges and ditches, returning fire on anyone who moved. Meanwhile, the machine gun teams set up their weapons where they stood and attempted to provide covering fire. The Battalion mortars did the same, firing indiscriminately in the direction of the German attack.

Despite the initial confusion, the Germans were equally as shocked to encounter such fierce opposition. Having swept aside one line of defence they had expected the road down to the river to be clear. Before long they began to retire in disorder. It had been a close call; if the 2/310th Infantry Regiment had arrived minutes later they would have been overrun, leaving the route to the bridge undefended.

310th Infantry Regiment advances onto Minderberg and Meerberg

As the 2/310th Infantry Regiment reorganised, the Regiment's 3rd Battalion and the 52nd Armored Infantry Battalion prepared to advance up the St Severinsberg valley. General Craig's plan was capture the twin peaks of Minderberg and Meerberg that overlooked Kretzhaus junction. General Craig is reported to have told his staff officers that they

> must expand in that direction to keep this from becoming a second Anzio beachhead.

As long as the two hills remained in German hands, they would continue to launch counterattacks against Ohlenberg, in the hope of reaching the river.

During the afternoon all three battalions advanced slowly towards their objectives along the steep wooded hillsides. 52nd Armoured Infantry Battalion advanced on the left, moving along the valley floor while the 3/310th Infantry Regiment filed along narrow paths through the woods. Although the 52nd did not encounter any troops, the battalion was periodically shelled as it picked its way forward. The 3/310th was not so lucky, snipers and mortars took their toll as the men climbed the hill. Occasionally German aircraft swooped low over the valley strafing the battalion. The advance continued, but casualties began to mount. A single bomb wiped out an entire squad of Company L and 'friendly' artillery fire decimated another squad.

While the two battalions threaded their way through the woods towards Meerberg, 2/310th had recovered from the shock of the German counterattack and reorganised ready to advance towards Minderberg. As the GIs made their way up the slope, they grimly counted the bodies left behind by the fierce firefight. However, they had little time to reflect on the fate of their comrades; as the lead squads left the outskirts of Ohlenberg they were subjected to a terrific mortar barrage. All four company commanders cajoled their men forward, yet dozens of men were killed or wounded by shrapnel, and the battalion had to fall back and regroup several times. Eventually Colonel Heyes' men managed to penetrate the woods north of Ohlenberg and as it grew dark they dug in close to the summit of Mindenberg. The battalion had suffered grievous losses during the day. Captain Hopkins of Company G had been seriously wounded while Company E had lost all but one of their officers.

Meanwhile, the two battalions heading towards the summit of Meerberg were still advancing slowly. 2/310th Infantry Regiment eventually reached its objective after a strenuous five hour march. Company K established a defensive position northeast of Ohlenberg, alongside 3/310th Infantry Regiment. A Panzer IV supported by machine guns blocked the road heading towards Kretzhaus. Although the Battalion had achieved one of its objectives, its position was far from secure. Company I dug in around the summit and tried to establish contact with the 52nd Armored Infantry Battalion to its left. All the time it was subjected to heavy artillery bombardments.

The two companies of the 52nd Armored Infantry Battalion

291st Engineer Combat Battalion completed the treadway bridge in record time. National Archives 111-SC-204629

had continued to make slow progress up the St Severinsberg valley but as it grew dark squad leaders found it increasingly difficult to keep their men together in the woods. Lieutenant-Colonel Prince's report describes what happened next:

> The companies moved up on their objective after dark, but due to complete darkness, intermittent artillery concentrations, breakdown in communications and doubt in the minds of the company commanders as to their positions, the troops were brought off the objective and marched back.

That withdrawal left 3/310th Infantry Regiment alone on Hill 448, with their left flank completely exposed. Fortunately, the Germans were completely unaware of the situation. By first light Companies A and B were back in their assembly area. Prince planned to send his men back up the valley, but orders from above cancelled the advance. The St Severinsberg valley offered few opportunities for exploitation, While Company C remained in place blocking the road into Kasbach, Companies A and C withdrew into reserve.

Despite the fact that 310th Infantry Regiment had managed to achieve some of its objectives, it was still a long way from securing Kretzhaus crossroads. As the GIs dug in on the steep slopes the Germans could be heard moving armour towards the junction. The battle for Kretzhaus was going to be a bitter drawn out duel.

The Battle for Dattenberg

At the southern tip of the bridgehead the 1st Battalion of the 310th Infantry Regiment had been ordered to capture Dattenberg on the last remaining ridge overlooking the Ludendorff Bridge. The plan was to attack three companies abreast. Company A would lead the centre of the attack into the heart of the village, while Company B scaled the heights to the northeast. Meanwhile, Company C would advance along the river road with three tanks to establish a roadblock facing Leubsdorf. Once the objectives had been taken tanks could set up roadblocks around Dattenberg.

Company B's advance north east of the village came under heavy fire from a 20mm AA battery dug in on the high ground. Infantry, armed with machine guns and panzerfausts, supported the battery and they were able to call on an impressive array of mortars and artillery. After suffering heavy casualties Company B withdrew to a safe distance and called for assistance. For the time being the rest of the battalion was fully engaged.

Company A had been able to advance unopposed through the centre of Dattenberg, however, Company C came under fire as soon as it they to move along the riverbank. The Germans were well dug in around a chateau on the slopes overlooking the road. Progress was slow and as 3rd Platoon reached the turn off to Dattenberg, Lieutenant Magura's tank ran over a mine, killing one of his crew. Men braved sniper fire to probe for further mines and the rest of the platoon gave covering fire to keep men armed with *Panzerfausts* at bay.

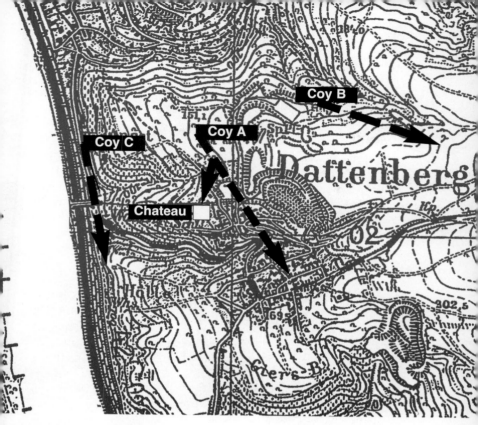

The Battle for Dattenberg.

It appeared that the chateau, a German headquarters and armoury, was the centre of resistance in Dattenberg. While C Company deployed a platoon on the slopes below the building to draw the Germans' fire, a platoon from Company A approached from the rear and stormed the gates of the building. A few Germans surrendered immediately but the majority sought refuge in the maze of corridors and rooms of the chateau. A nerve racking search followed but eventually 117 prisoners, many of them *Waffen SS* and paratroopers, were rounded up. The GIs also discovered an impressive arsenal of weapons; seventy-two machine guns and dozens of automatic rifles and machine pistols were found stored in the building. Huge stocks of small arms and ammunition were also uncovered.

Once the chateau had been cleared the infantry on the river

A radioman maintains traffic control on Erpel bridge.
National Archives 111-SC-411818

road were able to wave Captain Soumas' tanks on and while two blocked the river road the rest headed up the steep hill into Dattenberg. Two were posted on the southern outskirts of the village, covering the minor road into Leubsdorf; the rest were sent to assist Company B, pinned down north of the village.

As the tanks advanced along the Ronigerhof road, they were joined by a platoon of twelve men and a light machine gun squad for protection. East of the village the task force came under fire and while the tanks engaged in a furious battle with anti-tank guns, the infantry kept the German soldiers at bay. One intrepid German soldier armed with a *Panzerfaust* managed to creep up close to the tanks and, following a near miss, the infantry fanned out to deal with the future danger of that sort. Eventually, Private Alfredo Lavato managed to locate the German's position and after creeping close while under fire, he silenced the man with a grenade. The task force continued to push forward and as it approached the anti-aircraft battery, the crew surrendered.

Company B was eventually able to occupy the heights north east of Dattenberg, clearing the last ridge overlooking the Ludendorff Bridge. As they dug in, observers spotted a column of men and transport withdrawing along the valley to the southeast, having escaped from Dattenberg. Due to the fact that they had lost so many comrades earlier that day, the GIs showed no compassion. Opening fire they decimated the column.

1/310th Infantry Regiment had suffered heavy losses during the battle for Dattenberg, sixty men killed and wounded. In return they had captured over 150 prisoners and killed 85. As darkness fell, the last of Captain Soumas' tanks took up their positions covering the Ronigerhof road; Dattenberg was finally secure.

Work continues on the bridges along the river

While the ground troops expanded the bridgehead to deprive the Germans of the high ground overlooking the bridge, anti-aircraft batteries stationed along the valley were kept busy as the Luftwaffe tried time after time to bomb the bridge. Sixteen raids were made, five planes were shot down and another was damaged. The rest failed to hit the target. As each day passed the number of AA guns in the valley around Remagen was increasing, diminishing the German chances of destroying the Ludendorff Bridge.

Meanwhile, work on the treadway bridge at Erpel, was being delayed by the build up of traffic in the Remagen area. During the afternoon General Millikin visited Colonel Lyons to discuss the progress of the crossings and after hearing about the delays, instructed his staff to make sure the lorries carrying bridging equipment were given priority. 291st Engineer Battalion

General Millikin gave lorries carrying pontoons priority on the roads leading to Remagen. National Archives 111-SC-203733

eventually completed the 1032 feet long treadway bridge at 23:00, ready to open for traffic at first light. It was estimated that it had taken over 11,000 man hours to build what would become the longest tactical bridge of the war.

The start of the pontoon bridge at Linz had also been delayed. Although 1159th Engineer Combat Group had expected to start work at dusk on 9 March, the first pontoons did not start to arrive until the following afternoon. 181st and 552nd Engineer Heavy Pontoon Battalions worked throughout, floating pontoons out into the river while the 51st Combat Engineer Battalion positioned pneumatic floats to stabilise the bridge.

By now the majority of the hills overlooking the crossing were in American hands, reducing the threat from German artillery. It meant that Lieutenant-Colonel Harvey Fraser's men were able to work steadily throughout the night without interference.

CHAPTER TEN

THE ADVANCE THROUGH THE WESTERWALD BEGINS

Battle for Honnef

By 11 March, 311th Infantry Regiment had been in action for three days. Colonel Willingham's men were reaching the limits of endurance, yet General Craig expected him to hold his positions around Honnef, Mezenberg and Rheinbreitbach. The 11th *Panzer* Division was beginning to arrive in the area after three days and nights on the road and Willingham had been warned to expect to be counterattacked anytime. Roadblocks supported by armour and anti-tank guns covered the main roads through the town while infantry patrolled the streets in between. Colonel Willingham did not have to wait long. At first light the Germans struck 1st Battalion's positions near the river;

> An enemy counterattack in the Company C sector began at 06:50, when five enemy tanks accompanied by infantry drove down from Rhondorf to the northeast. Company C repulsed the attack and with the aid of artillery the enemy was quickly dispersed and knocked out. Again at 09:45 Company C received another counterattack coming south along the Rhine River. This attack consisted of four enemy tanks and infantry, but it too was smashed.

Further attacks continued throughout the afternoon and evening, but the 311th Infantry Regiment held its positions.

Supply trucks and ambulances head back across the river to Remagen.
National Archives 111-SC-235652

The advance towards Kretzhaus and Notscheid

By 11 March, Major-General Craig was confident that the bridgehead, was wide enough and turned his attentions to his next objective, cutting the highway running north to south through Kretzhaus and Notscheid. As long as the road remained in enemy hands the Germans would be able to distribute their reserves around the bridgehead. Kretzhaus crossroads was the key to the German position and as long as they held the road junction their armour could use the Bruchhausen and Ohlenberg roads to get to the river.

Unfortunately for General Craig, the terrain leading up to Kretzhaus and Notscheid was far from ideal. Wooded mountain sides and deep ravines prevented armour from leaving the two roads and the Germans could easily block the way forward with anti-tank guns. The rugged terrain would make it difficult to coordinate attacks and artillery support would find it hard to keep track of the infantry. Meanwhile, the Germans could wait on the high ground while their artillery and mortars shelled the valleys indiscriminately. One thing was becoming apparent, the fighting would be slow and costly. For once the Americans would not be able to bring their overwhelming numbers to bear in the cramped bridgehead.

At first light the 2nd Battalion of the 310th Infantry Regiment

A Tiger tank emerges from cover. Private William Lambert discouraged an attack by two of these monsters by the use of a bazooka.

Lifting the first pontoons into place on the Linz bridge. National Archives 111-SC-227274

left their foxholes and began to climb through the woods to the summit of Minderberg, overlooking Kretzhaus. As the troops advanced down the forward slope towards Kretzhaus mortars and self-propelled guns opened fire, pinning the battalion down. The tanks and tank destroyers that were supposed to support the attack ran into a strong anti-tank gun position and they were forced to retire back down the Ohlenberg road.

Before long the Germans retaliated driving Lieutenant-Colonel Culbreth's men back to the crest of Minderberg. Having dealt with 2nd Battalion's attack, the Germans turned their attentions on the Regiment's 3rd Battalion covering the Ohlenberg road. During the early afternoon seven tanks and several companies of infantry advanced down the road towards Company L and Company I. As the *panzers* crawled forward Private William F Lambert waited alongside the road with his bazooka. At a range of forty metres he opened fire hitting the lead Tiger tank. The *panzer MkVI* ground to a halt and, despite the fact that his bazooka shells were unable to penetrate the tank's armour, Lambert persisted. A second shot smacked into the stationary Tiger and then when Lambert had scored two more hits on a second Tiger, the column withdrew towards Kretzhaus.

Overnight all three battalions of the 47th Infantry Regiment had gathered in the vicinity of Ohlenberg ready to advance towards Notscheid. They faced a difficult task; the ground fell rapidly to the east of Ohlenberg and the twin peaks, Rennenberg I and Rennenberg II, towered over the Losbach valley. 1st Battalion advanced into the valley at 08:30 heading towards Rennenberg I but as soon as Company C began to descend into the valley it came under heavy fire. Company A A's attempts to outflank the German defensive positions also failed to make any headway. The 3rd Battalion advanced half an hour later with tank destroyers in close support and although it captured a number of strongpoints in Orbrunt, the Germans were determined to regain their positions,

> The enemy continued a determined resistance with small arms, artillery and tanks and it was not until 15:00 hours that the objective including the houses at 690215 [Orbrunt] were cleared out. Forty-four prisoners were taken in the engagement and two enemy tanks were destroyed by our Tank Destroyers.

2nd Battalion's advance north of Ohlenberg was also checked, stifling 47th Infantry Regiment's hopes for a rapid advance towards Notscheid.

Air attacks
While the battle raged on in the hills east of the river, the Luftwaffe continued to carry sorties against the Ludendorff

The crew of the first halftrack mounted AA gun to cross the Rhine keep a lookout for German planes. National Archives 111-SC-361065

Bridge. The raid on 7 March started at 07:30 when three planes, one He111, a Me109 and a FW190 were shot down as they swooped low over the river. During the afternoon five more planes flew down the valley through a curtain of anti-aircraft fire. Two FW190s were shot down and the rest were forced to abort their mission, pulling away in the face of intense flak. Later on two FW190s and an Me109 appeared in the skies over Remagen and after circling 12,000 feet to study their target dived in low on their bombing run, but again the flak was too intense. The pilots were forced to take evasive action as they came under fire, and all three bombs that they released missed their target. 413 Automatic Anti-aircraft Battery's daily summary details the tactics used by the Luftwaffe;

> *The enemy operated seventeen raiders, singly and in pairs, over the REMAGEN Bridge and bridgehead through the daylight hours. Heeding the lesson learned the previous day, the enemy aircraft took more evasive action and did more manoeuvring prior to bombing runs and flew at lower altitudes. The desperation of the Luftwaffe was again indicated in the variety of aircraft used – FW190's Me109's, Me210's, He111's, Me262's and one AR234 were reported during this period. The highlight of the day was when one 90mm gun section of the 413 AAA Gun Battalion engaged an Me210 with a single pre-cut round of ammunition and claimed the aircraft destroyed.*

However, some pilots appeared to be under orders to reach the bridge at all costs. At 17:00 the crews of 413 Automatic Anti-aircraft Battery watched in amazement as eight Stukas flew down the valley at 3,000 feet, refusing to take evasive action they came under fire; none of them survived.

Completing the Linz Pontoon Bridge

General Millikin was pleased to hear that the treadway bridge at Erpel had been opened for traffic at dawn on 11 March. Meanwhile, work had progressed steadily overnight on the pontoon bridge at Linz:

> *The night of the 10th was the night that some of our boys really went through hell for the first time. Our Battalion was working near the Remagen Bridge trying to put in a Bailey Bridge and was forced to stop due to heavy artillery by the enemy. Some of our boys from the section whose job it was to be*

Traffic files across the Linz bridge, the Kaiserberg overshadows the town.
National Archives 111-SC-203738

on the bridge at that time helped the wounded and evacuated
them under fire. None of those men of this company suffered any
injuries. The company was proud of each and everyone who
helped.

Although Lieutenant-Colonel Harvey Fraser was confident
that he would have the bridge finished on time, during the
morning disaster struck. A landing craft broached in the fast
current and it was swept into the bridge, completely wrecking
a span near the east bank; it took seven hours to repair the
damage. Finally at 22:00 Fraser was able to report that the
pontoon bridge was open for traffic. Now that troops could
now cross at Linz, it relieved the bottleneck south of the
Ludendorff Bridge. General Millikin was now confident that
he could keep the bridgehead supplied with men and
equipment and overnight Colonel Lyons was allowed to close
the railway bridge for repairs.

CHAPTER ELEVEN

THE BATTLE FOR
KRETZHAUS AND NOTSCHEID

Attempts to push east to cut the road passing through Kretzhaus and Notscheid continued on 12 March 1945 in the face of fierce resistance. Major Henry H Hardenbergh had taken over command of the 2/310th Infantry Regiment after Lieutenant-Colonel Culbreth had been evacuated with battle fatigue. Hardenbergh's men had spent a weary night being shelled and mortared on the crest of Meerberg and at 06:45 they advanced a second time towards Kretzhaus. The intention was to establish a roadblock north of the village but, once again, they came under heavy fire from infantry and tank fire as they moved through the woods. For several hours Companies F and G crept forward across the rough terrain, until they were close to the Bruchhausen road junction, northwest of Kretzhaus. Just as Major Hardenbergh thought he had managed to take his objective, a company of infantry and four *panzer* Mk IV tanks counterattacked and broke into Company F's position.

Fighting at close range, Hardenburg's men managed to drive

German infantry move up behind a Panzer Mk IV.

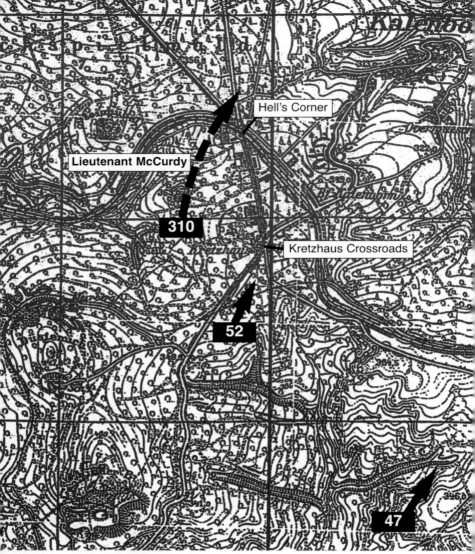

The attack on Kretzhaus.

off the counterattack before withdrawing a short distance from the vulnerable position. His force now spent, Major Hardenburg handed over his positions to the 52nd Armored Infantry Battalion overnight. The battalion had been expecting to take over Kretzhaus crossroads, instead, Lieutenant-Colonel Prince found that he would have to launch an attack to capture it at first light.

As 310th Infantry Regiment fought its way towards Kretzhaus, 47th Infantry Regiment tried once more to advance across the Losbach valley. At midday Colonel Smythe was pleased to hear that his 1st Battalion had reached the summit of Rennenberg I, and despite heavy fire from several directions, it had managed to establish a defensive perimeter. The capture of the hill meant that troops could pass safely along the Kretzhaus road for the first time. The 2nd Battalion managed to advance some distance along the road, but it soon came under heavy artillery and mortar fire directed from Rennenberg II. Colonel Smythe's men would have to take the hill before he could hope to cut the road between Kretzhaus and Notscheid.

The following morning 310th Infantry Regiment launched another attack on the village. The 52nd Armored Infantry Battalion was expected to advance along the Ohlenberg road, driving the Germans back towards Kalenborn. A platoon of Sherman tanks and a platoon of tank destroyers would support the battalion, however, Lieutenant-Colonel Prince was expecting to meet fierce opposition. At least two Tiger tanks and four Panzer IVs had been spotted prowling around Kretzhaus; the following note sums up the respect shown by Prince towards his adversary:

> Not that the enemy was present in any particular strength, but he had the high ground, and he made the best use of it, his tanks and machine guns being very carefully and effectively placed.

The Germans were determined to push the Americans back into the Rhine.

Accurate artillery and mortar fire greeted Companies A and B as they drew close to Kretzhaus and a number of machine gun nests made it impossible to reach the crossroads. Both company commanding officers, lieutenants Eugene Biondi and Maurice Deal, were wounded and although the infantry looked to the armour for support, the tank destroyers were experiencing their own difficulties:

> One of the Tigers was sitting astride the crossroads in the village, firing down the approach routes. A stiff fight developed. Every time a house was cleared the enemy launched a counterattack. The companies finally succeeded in capturing about a third of the town; then they dug in to hold what they had.

In an effort to reinforce his position, Lieutenant-Colonel Prince ordered Company C forward. When Captain Wortham reached the front line he realised that it was impossible to make a frontal attack. The only option open was to try and outflank the German positions. Second Lieutenant William McCurdy was ordered to take his platoon to the north, cutting through the woods to avoid detection. His men spotted a number of machine gun nests as they approached the Bruchhausen road and a Panzer IV was sat squarely on the junction covering the approach roads. Lieutenant-Colonel Prince's report vividly describes how Lieutenant McCurdy's men assaulted the position:

> This officer led his platoon of 28 men in an attack up the road through woods towards the tank. Upon closer approach he definitely spotted the tank, and by means of radio adjusted Tank Destroyer fire on the tank and surrounding positions. This tank returned fire with both 75mm and calibre 31 machine gun, but only succeeded in wounding two men in Lt McCurdy's platoon. The enemy was knocked out without further casualties to our men. Lt McCurdy then continued his advance and with assault fire cleared out the woods and reached his objective. Two additional enemy tanks were located 440 yards to the northwest and northeast but were knocked out as TD fire was again directed on them. Four additional men were seriously wounded on the objective by enemy 88mm fire from the tanks. By the time the force reached the crossroads there were only 12 men left of the 28. This place was nicknamed 'Hell's Corner' by the men of the 52nd.

Lieutenant McCurdy's bold advance had succeeded in cutting the road north of the Kretzhaus. Throughout the evening the rest of Captain Wortham's men worked alongside 3/310th Infantry Regiment to clear infantry from the woods while tank destroyers moved up to form roadblocks in front of the village.

To the southeast, the two battalions of the 47th Infantry Regiment continued to push forward towards Notscheid in the face of fierce resistance. Tanks and infantry checked 2nd Battalion's advance up the Losbach valley and the 1st Battalion attempts to penetrate the village failed. However, by nightfall the Regiment had managed to establish a firing line over looking the road between Kretzhaus and Notscheid. The two battalions brought up their reserve companies and continued to advance slowly under cover of darkness, reaching the road by dawn. For the first time the Germans were unable to move their reinforcements freely between the two villages.

14 March was a day of reorganisation as the 310th Infantry Regiment prepared for its final assault on Kretzhaus and by first light it had established a continuous line facing the village. Meanwhile, 47th Regiment's 1st Battalion came under heavy fire as it tried once more to reach Notscheid. *Panzers*, self propelled guns and machine guns made sure that nothing could get within 400 metres of the village. Although the 60th Armored Infantry Battalion had managed to advance from the south to get within striking distance of Notscheid, the Germans were determined to hold the village for as long as possible.

At dawn on 15 March five battalions launched an attack across the road that had served as the main axis for German

GIs share a soft drink during a lull in the fighting. National Archives 111-SC-421486

reserves for the past week. Two companies of the 3/310th Infantry Regiment advanced into Kretzhaus under heavy fire and after Company I crossed the road south of the crossroads Lieutenant Herman J Carlson led his platoon into woods south of the village. The regimental history describes what he found:

> In the woods they discovered four enemy tanks supported by infantry. Dropping in the woods were mortar and artillery shells. But the infantry got close to the tanks, so close the tanks couldn't fire on them. Close enough so that two men were injured by muzzle blasts from the tanks' guns. They stuck there until the enemy infantry were driven back. Then the rifle support backed up so the bazookamen could fire at the tanks, which, although only slightly damaged, withdrew.

Having driven off the tanks, Company I was able to clear the houses around the crossroads, allowing tanks to come forward and clear the railway station and the woods beyond. Lieutenant-Colonel Lutz had been in the thick of the fighting throughout the day but as he reconnoitred the battalion's next objective the Regimental Command Post received the codeword 'Punt, Pass, Pray'; it mean that Lutz had been wounded. Despite the setback, Captain Olson led Company I east towards Kalenborn and with the help of a company from the 52nd Armored Infantry Battalion his men captured the road network overlooking Kalenborn.

After five days of bitter fighting, 'Hell's Corner' was finally secure and as the GIs began to dig in they couldn't fail to notice the burnt out German halftracks and tanks littering the woods. The 52nd Armored Infantry Battalion alone suffered over two hundred casualties in the battle for Kretzhaus. There is no record of how many German soldiers lost their lives in the battle.

To the southeast, 47th Infantry Regiment eventually entered Notscheid and with the help of the 60th Armored Infantry Battalion secured the village by nightfall. It meant that General Millikin held a continuous front between Kalenborn and Notscheid; the Remagen bridgehead was finally secure. Now that he had control of the road network through the Westerwald, he would be able to build up his own reserves ready to advance across the autobahn connecting Cologne and Frankfurt.

CHAPTER TWELVE

ATTACKS ON THE BRIDGE CONTINUE

Security at the Bridge

Air attacks continued intermittently after the bridge closed for repairs; fortunately the increase in anti-aircraft units along the banks of the Rhine made it impossible for planes to make accurate bombing runs. Even so, III Corps was conscious that it was still reliant on the temporary bridges. If the Germans managed to destroy one or more of the bridges, the operations on the east bank would be seriously hampered. There were concerns that the Germans might try sabotage and to counter the threat a number of preventative measures were put in place:

On both sides of the river, above and below the bridges, 155 howitzers direct fire, tanks, tank destroyers, assault guns and numerous automatic weapons are covering the river approaches.

Booms were positioned to prevent the Germans floating mines down the river. National Archives 111-SC-351173

Powerful searchlights were used to stop saboteurs reaching the bridges.
National Archives 111-SC-407119

Evacuating the local population to temporary camps. National Archives 111-SC-202362

LCVPs are on call to tow large floating craft ashore. Depth charges used at irregular intervals are another protective measure being used against attacks by swimmers, small submarines, floating mines or other similar devices. A system of lights and patrol boats is also used on the river to aid in the detection of possible attacks by water. Booms have also been placed above and below the bridges and nets are being hung as rapidly as possible as another means of preventing attacks by swimmers, submersibles or mines. At the bridge approaches guards are maintaining a check of unidentified vehicles to prevent the possibility of sabotage by trucks loaded with explosives or incendiaries.

III Corps Intelligence was aware that artillery observers may well have infiltrated behind the American lines, hiding out on the wooded hills. Radio nets were constantly monitored to try and locate their positions, while reconnaissance vehicles patrolled the area. The front line troops took the precaution by evacuating civilians from areas of high ground overlooking the river.

Despite the security measures, during the early hours of 16 March seven German frogmen tried to reach the east bank of the river. The plan was to swim down to the bridge, pushing explosive charges strapped onto small floats before them. The first attempt had to be cancelled due to artillery fire, however the frogmen returned the following night. One by one they slipped into the icy waters of the Rhine and began swimming towards one of the pontoon bridges. They did not get far before powerful searchlights spotted them. Four managed to escape but the rest were captured and taken for questioning.

First Army's report shows the variety of sabotage methods considered by the Germans:

> *Preliminary interrogation of three swimming saboteurs captured early this morning in an attempt to destroy bridges*

A German Frogman, captured as he tried to swim to the bridge. National Archives 111-SC-207478

143

across the Rhine disclosed that this attempt will probably be followed by others of varying character including swimmers with torpedos, mines, etc. German navy units are in the area operating with these saboteurs who were trained by SKORENZY the German master saboteur.

The Luftwaffe persists and the Germans use V2 rockets

Poor weather prevented air attacks on the morning of 12 March but the skies over Remagen came alive once more during the afternoon. Forty-seven planes tried to bomb the bridge, many of them diving out of low clouds to the north and west. Most flew alone, braving the ring of anti-aircraft batteries positioned on either side of the river. Casualties were enormous. Twenty-three planes were shot down and five others were badly damaged. The following report sums up the air defences protecting the Ludendorff Bridge:

In the old days the flak defences of Happy Valley were the most intense encountered by our air force. Today most of the enemy flak in the Rhine and Ruhr is gone, but the gun sites are not vacant. In the REMAGEN bridge area the flak curtain put up by our anti-aircraft men is heavy enough to do handsprings

Anti-aircraft guns line the banks of the river. National Archives 111-SC-380371

974th P Squadron of the Royal Air Force stationed barrage baloons near the bridge. Leroy/Friedensmuseum

on. *The enemy pilots are rapidly becoming aware of this, and the title of this sector can now be changed to 'Happy, Happy Valley'.*

Although there was little chance of eliminating the bridgehead by 13 March, the Luftwaffe still persisted in carrying out attacks along the Rhine. As well as targeting the Ludendorff Bridge, attempts were made to destroy the temporary bridges but the number of anti-aircraft batteries surrounding Remagen was rising daily, making it increasingly difficult to fly anywhere near the river. II Corps would eventually have sixteen 90mm AA batteries and twenty-five other batteries of a smaller calibre around Remagen. The area would eventually be covered by the largest concentration of air defences assembled during the war.

The number of attacks on any of the bridges began to diminish as the bridgehead grew. There were only thirteen raids on 13 March, all carried out by the jet-propelled Me262; three were shot down and the rest failed to register a hit. The following day there were nine raids, and the pilots resorted to evasive tactics, weaving about at high level as they dropped their bombs. Again they failed to cause any significant damage. Over the course of nine days, 367 planes attacked the Rhine crossings. 109 were shot down and a further thirty-six unconfirmed kills were reported.

Shortly after the bridge had been captured, the Germans brought forward a panzer-mounted Karl Howitzer artillery

Keeping watch for enemy planes as engineers build another bridge across the Rhine. National Archives 111-SC-360970

piece, a huge weapon weighing in at 132 tonnes. The tank was capable of firing a 4,400 pound shell, but it malfunctioned after firing a handful of rounds and had to be withdrawn.

The German threat of air raids had begun to diminish but they were about to launch another menace on Remagen – their V Weapons.

The first report of V rockets in the Remagen area was made on 14 March by 413 Automatic Anti-Aircraft Battery. Observers believed that a single V1 Flying Bomb had been fired towards the bridgehead. However, the V1 was unsuitable for a target as small as the Ludendorff Bridge. The flying bomb was designed to fly on a set course until its fuel ran out and despite the fact that it had been able to wreak havoc on English cities over the past twelve months, there was little chance of it damaging one of the Rhine crossings. The V2 was far more sophisticated, relying on gyroscopes and electronics to guide it towards its target. The weapon was in its infancy but so far it had only been used on large strategic targets. Hitler ordered them to be used against Remagen, (it would be the only occasion that the V2 would be used in a tactical role). Three V2s were fired on 14 March from a base at Deventer in Holland and they all landed some distance away from Remagen. The following morning 413 AAA Battery's observer spotted two more being launched and watched as they tore out of sight into the atmosphere:

At 06:15am a vapour trail, rising vertically from the ground was observed through a director telescope while a net message was being run. At 06:45 the same was again observed. It is believed that the trails were from V2s.

Later, a number of reconnaissance planes were spotted circling over Remagen trying to find out if the V2s had hit their intended target. They returned to base disappointed. A further four

Work begins on a pontoon bridge connecting Remagen to Unkel. National Archives 111-SC-336971

rockets were launched on the morning of 17 March and 413 AAA Battery managed to track them as they approached:

> At 09:55 hrs, while tracking two planes, at 9,500ft, flying from west to east, Battery B observed four objects resembling bombs pass across the tracker telescopes. The objects fell in a direction east to west. Several large explosions, at least two were heard at the same time. Small pieces of aluminium scraps fell, some in the Battery position.

The missile in question had landed in the hills east of Ockenfels, two miles east of the bridge. The others landed in the hills surrounding Remagen. Another rocket, launched a few hours later came close to destroying the bridge.

> While examining the railroad bridge, the men at a 40mm gun section were questioned and told of a double explosion at about 12:30hrs. They had a piece of heavy aluminium which fell with ice on it immediately after the explosion.

The rocket had exploded on the east bank of the river, between Erpel and Unkel, within a few hundred metres of the bridge. That afternoon two more rockets were fired and landed miles from the target. One landed ten miles to the northwest while the second exploded in the hills east of Linz.

A second crossing at Remagen allowed the engineers to close the Ludendorff Bridge. National Archives 111-SC-234525

Chapter Thirteen

COLLAPSE OF THE BRIDGE

Engineers attempt to repair the Ludendorff Bridge

The German demolition explosion on 7 March had failed to destroy the Ludendorff Bridge, but it had severely crippled the thirty-year-old structure.

As troops began to cross to the Rhine, engineers from the 9th Armored Engineer Battalion had removed packages of explosives that had failed to detonate from the superstructure. A later inspection by the 276th Engineer Combat Battalion revealed that the Germans had filled manholes in the bridge piers with devices. They too had failed to explode.

As the endless convoy of men and vehicles crossed the Rhine, engineers began to carry out emergency repairs to make the bridge as safe as possible. The decking could be repaired, the damage to the upstream truss made it unsafe to open the bridge to two-way traffic. III Corps report vividly describes the extent of the damage done by the explosion:

... [it] had completely torn apart the lower chord, diagonal, and vertical of the truss at the first panel point south of the north pier. As a result of this, the upstream arch truss had dropped at the north end over one foot below the level of the downstream arch truss at the corresponding point. The side plates of the top chord of this upstream truss directly above the point where the lower chord was cut were slightly buckled.

The downstream girders supported the whole weight of the bridge and the tremendous stresses imposed by the twisted superstructure had caused several girders to deform under the strain.

Despite the engineers' concerns, General Millikin could ill afford to close the bridge until alternative crossings had been opened to traffic. The treadway bridge at Erpel had been opened for traffic on 10 March and the Linz pontoon bridge was completed the following day. A second crossing at Remagen was finished soon afterwards. Confident that he could keep the bridgehead supplied with men and equipment, Millikin allowed his Chief Engineer, Colonel Lyons, to close the

Ludendorff Bridge for repairs on 12 March.

The 276th Combat Engineer Battalion immediately began work on the crippled bridge with the help of 1058th Port Construction and Repair Group's technical team. The first priority was to repair the decking to allow their equipment to move freely along the bridge. Lieutenant-Colonel Clayton Rust's men began by cutting and welding the damaged hangers that supported the decking. The torn floor girders were then trimmed and spliced so that new timbers could be laid across the gap. On 17 March Lieutenant-Colonel Rust was ready to begin work on the broken lower chord, adjacent to the north abutment. Once it had been repaired both arches would once again, support the bridge. Colonel Rust's report illustrates the problems faced by his engineers:

> The crane was on the bridge over the north pier with a cable attached which ran through a block on the downstream side of the bridge, through the deck to another block and across under the deck to the part of the bottom chord of the upstream truss which framed into the pier. Attempts to take up on this cable were made once but the clamps slipped...

As the engineers went in search of new clamps, Captain Francis Goodwin of the 1159th Engineer Combat Group walked across the bridge to inspect the continuing repair work. Men were beginning to clear spare timber from the decking, loading the smaller pieces onto a truck while stacking others alongside the pedestrian walkway. Meanwhile, Major Carr was supervising repairs to the decking, next to the idle crane. Captain Goodwin mounted his motorcycle on the east bank, but as he rode towards Erpel a distant rumbling caught his attention:

> Just prior to crossing the treadway bridge, I heard an unusual sound and looking up saw that the arch of the bridge had just crumbled and the abutment section was settling to the ground. The time was 15:00.

Ten days, almost to the hour since the first American troops had crossed the Rhine, the Ludendorff Bridge collapsed into the river.

Lieutenant-Colonel Rust was at the centre of the bridge with his assistant, Captain Sergi when the bridge began to show signs that it was about to collapse:

> The first idea I had of any trouble was a sharp report like a rivet head shearing and I noticed a vertical hanger which had

'I knew instantly that the bridge was collapsing and I turned towards the south bank and ran as fast as I could.'

been spliced by two turnbuckles was breaking loose and one turnbuckle was dangling, having come loose at the top of the turnbuckle. It appeared as though the bolt holding the turnbuckle to the web of the vertical member had sheared through the web. At that instant I heard another sharp report of a rivet shearing off from my left rear followed by a trembling sensation of the whole deck. Quickly glancing down the deck, the whole deck seemed to be vibrating and dust was coming off the surface. I knew instantly that the bridge was collapsing and I turned towards the

'...the bridge fell into the Rhine at 15:00 hrs, carrying men with it.'

Searching for the injured amongst the debris. National Archives 111-SC-202821

south bank and ran as fast as I could. While I was running, the east side of the bridge seemed to settle first and I found myself running, in effect 'on a side hill'. The next instant I was engulfed in water. I had no sensation of falling at all.

The two officers were swept downstream and were finally rescued at the treadway bridge. Although both men escaped with minor injuries, many others were killed or injured. As ambulances gathered around the wreckage, men dived into the Rhine to try and rescue injured men from the strong current. Power boats operating in the Linz area, were sent downstream to assist the rescue operation.

As the afternoon wore on the number of casualties grew as men were pulled from the wreckage. The 276th Engineer Combat Battalion suffered the greatest loss: six men were killed outright and eleven were missing, sixty had been injured, three of them fatally. The 1058th Port and Construction Repair Unit lost eight men; another six were injured.

St Patrick's Day. This was the blackest day in the history of

Medics evacuate the casualties to safety. National Archives 111-SC-202822

the 1058th Engr. P.C. & R. and no man will forget it. After learning of three casualties at the Ludendorff Bridge yesterday we did learn today that the bridge fell into the Rhine at 15:00 hrs, carrying men with it.

As the medics struggled to extricate the injured, everyone began to wonder why the Ludendorff Bridge had finally crumbled into the Rhine.

Although III Corps investigation could not pinpoint the exact cause of the collapse, the report pointed to a number of possible contributory factors. The initial explosion on the afternoon of 7 March had left the downstream truss supporting the full weight of the bridge and it should have been enough to bring it crashing down into the river. German attempts to destroy the structure over the days that followed could have added to the stresses in the girders. Although only a handful of shell bursts had struck the superstructure, over 600 rounds had landed in close proximity to the bridge; a V2 rocket had also exploded close by a few hours before it collapsed.

However, III Corps had also contributed to the stresses and strains placed on the Ludendorff Bridge. Between the 7th and 12 March, thousands of men and dozens of lorries and tanks had flowed almost continuously across the bridge. Additional timber decking added by engineers to allow the vehicles to cross had increased the loading on the bridge by fifty tonnes according to conservative estimates. A number of heavy artillery batteries had been moved into the Remagen area to support the bridgehead and during the course of ten days eight inch howitzers had fired over one thousand rounds. The repair work to the upstream truss, in progress at the time of collapse, may have also been a significant factor.

Whatever the reason, the Ludendorff Bridge had served its purpose as far as the Allied High Command was concerned and

Ambulances line up along the east bank of the river. National Archives 111-SC-336971

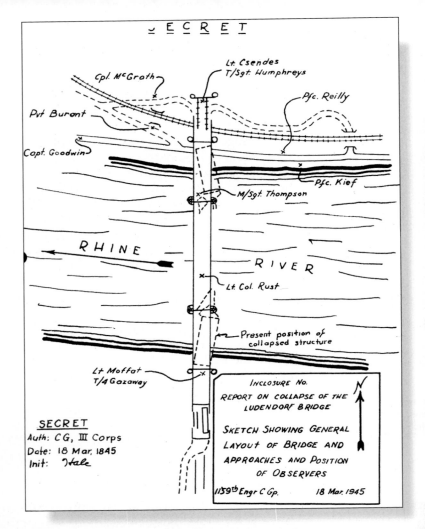

Sketch of the collapsed bridge and the position of witnesses.

an in depth inquiry would have served no purpose. III Corps
Report sums up the evidence;

> ...it must be assumed that the bridge collapsed from a
> combination of causes which, when added together finally proved
> the straw to 'break the camel's back'.

A short time after the bridge collapsed, General Bradley called
General Millikin to tell that he had bad news, he was to be
replaced by General Van Fleet. For some time both he and
General Hodges had been unsatisfied with the way Millikin had

'...it must be assumed that the bridge collapsed from a combination of causes..' National Archives 111-SC-331838

With Remagen bridge collapsed into the Rhine 9th Armored Division's sign was defunct. Lewis E Thurston/Friedenmuseum

Hitler's expectation: How the Ludendorff bridge should have looked when the Americans reached the banks of the Rhine at Remagen.

handled the expansion of the bridgehead and he considered that his subordinate had let an opportunity slip away. In Bradley's words:

> *I have only the greatest respect for the GIs doing the fighting out there, but I think they have had bad leadership in this bridgehead battle.*

Millikin in turn had bad news, reporting the collapse of the Ludendorff Bridge. Despite the loss of the rail bridge, the temporary bridges across the Rhine were more than adequate to sustain the bridgehead.

When Millikin's replacement, General Van Fleet, took command of III Corps on 17 March the crisis was over. The Remagen bridgehead had succeeded in drawing German reserves from other vital sectors along the Rhine, in particular 21 Army Group's chosen crossing point between Emmerich and Wesel, to the northwest of Düsseldorf. Field Marshal Montgomery was in the final stages of preparing to launch Operations Plunder and Varsity, a river crossing on 23 March, followed by an airborne assault the following day. The attack would stand far a greater chance of success due to the capture of the Bridge at Remagen.

Court martialling those responsible for the capture of the Remagen bridge

While the fighting raged throughout the Westerwald, Hitler was venting his anger against the men responsible for the debacle. He was infuriated that the Americans had managed to cross the Rhine; the capture of the Ludendorff Bridge had denied his Armies the chance to regroup behind the river. After replacing von Rundstedt with Kesselring, Hitler appointed *Leutnant-general* Rudolf Hübner to lead a team of officers to court-martial those responsible. The fact that the interrogators were to be accompanied by an execution squad left no one in any doubt what the sentence would be for those found guilty.

After questioning a number of senior Generals, Hübner went on to interrogate the NCOs and men who had been at the bridge on 7 March. The results of the investigation led to verdicts being decided against the two captured officers, Captain Bratge and Captain Friesenhahn. Bratge was found guilty of failing to carry out his orders and was sentenced to death in his absence while Friesenhahn was acquitted, having done everything within his powers to try and destroy the bridge.

Adolf Hitler was furious at the news that the Americans had captured the Remagen bridge. He took immediate action against those he considered resposible.

Feldmarschall Gerd von Rundstedt. Sacked.

On the morning of 13 March the court arrived in Rimbach to try Major Scheller and *Leutnant* Peters. Hübner was in no doubt about Scheller's guilt on two counts. Firstly, he had delayed the issuing of the order to destroy the bridge while the second charge accused Scheller of abandonding the men under his command. Although he had escaped to report the news to the

Scheller   Peters   Kraft   Strobel

The men who paid with their lives for failures at Remagen bridge.

nearest headquarters, the court concluded that he should have taken steps to launch a counterattack while there were only a few Americans on the east bank of the Rhine. *Leutnant* Peters was also tried and found guilty of allowing his experimental anti-aircraft guns fall into enemy hands. Both men were taken out into the woods and shot.

During the afternoon the court moved to Oberirsen to try Major Strobel, the commanding officer of engineering works along the Rhine, and Major Kraft, Friesenhahn's superior officer. Both men were found guilty of failing to organise successful counterattacks against the bridgehead on the night of 7 March. Strobel was also charged with neglecting the communications network connecting Remagen to his headquarters. The following morning both men were sentenced to death and executed.

Apart from von Rundstedt, four other senior Generals were blamed for the capture of the Ludendorff Bridge and removed from their positions. General von Bothmer, the unfortunate officer placed in command of the Remagen district hours before the bridge was captured was sentenced to five years imprisonment; he committed suicide a few days later.

CHAPTER FOURTEEN

TOURING REMAGEN AND THE WESTERWALD

Travelling to Remagen

Remagen is situated between Bonn, twenty miles to the north, and Koblenz, thirty miles to the south. Visitors travelling by car from the northwest will approach the area along Autobahn E31. Take exit 30, signposted **Bad Neuenahr** and **Ahrweiler** and follow road number **573** south for three kilometres (2 miles). On the outskirts Bad Neuenahr take road number **266** heading east, signposted for **Sinzig** and Remagen (a new section of bypass is due to open soon, so follow signs carefully). Just beyond the Sinzig turn off take the Remagen exit at the roundabout, heading north along Route 9. Remagen town centre is signposted to the right after one mile.

Visitors travelling by road from Bonn need to head south along Route 9. The road follows the west bank of the Rhine, providing spectacular views of the Rhineland. Remagen is twenty miles south of the city. Visitors heading north from Koblenz, again follow Route 9 and after the road bypasses Andernach, the road hugs the west bank of the river. Exits for Remagen are to the right after thirty miles.

Remagen stands on the main rail link between Köln (Cologne), Bonn and Koblenz and most trains between the cities stop at the town. An alternative way of reaching the area for those wishing to leave their car at home is to fly. Many airlines serve Köln/Bonn airport for a reasonable price. The flight is between 60 and 90 minutes. A shuttle bus service takes passengers to Bonn railway station (*Bahnhof*) for five euros (at the time of writing). There is a regular train service between Bonn and Remagen and a one-way journey costs about four euros and takes no more than thirty minutes.

Staying in Remagen

Although there are a wide variety of hotels to choose from in Remagen, in the summer months in can be a popular location for tourists visiting the Rhineland. There are also a number of festivals in the area and again the town can be busy. The list of hotels given below is not comprehensive and prices vary according to the facilities on offer:

Hotel-Restaurant Fährhaus
Rheinallee 23
53424 Remagen-Kripp
Tel.: 02642-44213
Fax: 02642-45214

Hotel-Restaurant Rhein-Ahr
Quellenstrasse 67-69
53424 Remagen-Kripp
Tel.: 02642-44112
Fax: 02642-46319

Hotel-Restaurant Rheingold-Ahrmünde
Rheinallee 3-4
53424 Remagen-Kripp
Tel.: 02642-44410
Fax: 02642-43462

Hotel-Restaurant Anker
Rheinpromenade 40
53424 Remagen
Tel.: 02642-23377
Fax: 02642-23377

Hotel-Restaurant Rhineland-Holiday
Gschwister-Scholl-Strasse 1
53424 Remagen
Tel.: 02642-93840
Fax: 02642-9384690

Hotel Garni Pinger 'Old Inn'
Gschwister-Scholl-Strasse 8
53424 Remagen
Tel.: 02642-93840
Fax: 02642-9384690

Hotel-Restaurant Boulevard
Bahnhofsstrasse 3
53424 Remagen
Tel.: 02642-23935
Fax: 02642-23935

Vita-Hotel Curanum
Alte Strasse 42-46
53424 Remagen
Tel.: 02642-2070
Fax: 02642-207999

It is possible to hire bicycles in Remagen, either at the railway station or at the Hotel Pinger (Rhineland Holiday) opposite the station. Daily rates are approximately eight euros. The kompass 1:50,000 Wander-und Radtourkarte covering Bonn and Ahrtal, Reference number 820, is ideal for finding your way around the Remagen area.

Car Tour 1
Meckenheim to Remagen - *45 minutes*

This tour covers the ground crossed by Combat Command B as it advanced towards the Rhine on the morning of 7 March 1945.

Meckenheim railway station, starting point of Tour 1.

Meckenheim railway station (1), on the northern outskirts of the town, serves as the starting point for the tour. If at any point you become lost, head into the centre of Meckenheim and look for signs for, or ask for, the *Bahnhof* (railway station).

Visitors coming from the northwest or from Koblenz to the south along the A61, need to take exit 10, signposted for Rheinbach. Those coming from the northwest need to turn left at the bottom of the slip road, those coming from the south take a right turn. Turn right at the T-junction after ½ mile, signposted for Meckenheim and railway station is on the left after a mile. Turn right into the town at the traffic lights outside the station (signposted for Adendorf and Alt Meckenheim).

Visitors approaching from the direction of Bonn or Köln (Cologne), head south along the A565, exiting the autobahn at

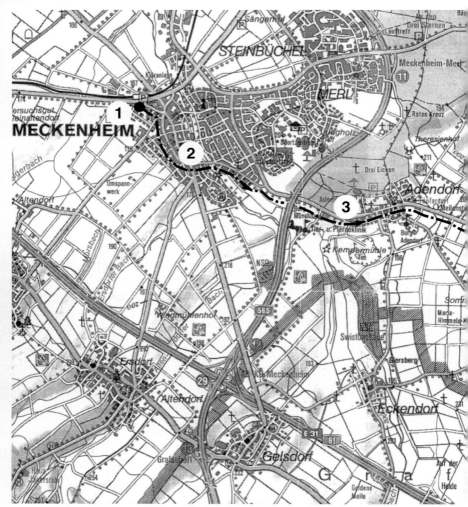

Your drive, or cycle ride, from Meckenheim to Berkum.

junction 10, Meckenheim-Nord. Continue in a southwest direction and after two miles turn left at the traffic lights in front of the station (signposted for Adendorf and Alt Meckenheim).

This tour covers the ground crossed by Combat Command B as it advanced towards the Rhine on the morning of 7 March 1945. Although it follows the road taken by the northern column, and the men who would make the initial crossing of the bridge at Remagen, it is possible to view large sections of southern column's route as it headed towards Sinzig and the River Ahr.

Head south along Bahnhofstrasse, passing the Rathuis (Town Hall) on your left, and after 250 metres, turn right at the small

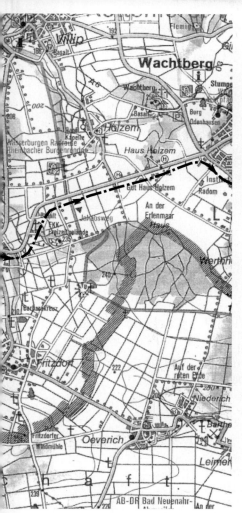

roundabout into and then proceed onto Klosterstrasse, following the sign for Adendorf. This road by-passes the centre of the town, which is to your left. As there are only a few shops on the road to Remagen, it may be prudent to find off street parking and buy any provisions you require.

The 27th Armored Infantry Battalion captured Stadt Meckenheim on the afternoon of 6 March and billeted in the town overnight. Bombing raids by the USAF had reduced large parts of the town to ruins, blocking many of the streets with rubble. The divisional engineers had worked through night to clear a way through the debris, however, Task Force Engeman was delayed by two hours.

Continuing south along Klosterstrasse, then head straight on when you reach the roundabout, signposted for Adendorf (2). A military police patrol waited at this junction (a crossroads in 1945) on the morning of 7 March, ready to redirect the southern column. The 52nd Armored Infantry Battalion, was supposed to follow the Adendorf road, however, Brigadier Hoge's new orders redirected the column to the right towards Gelsdorf and Eckendorf.

Head up the slope through the suburbs, turning right at the traffic lights at the top of the hill, signposted for Bad Goesburg and Adendorf. After passing under the autobahn bridge, the countryside opens up to the right and it is possible to see

The northern column captured the 5th Panzer Army Storm Battalion in Adendorf.

Eckendorf, the southern column's new objective, in the distance. Meanwhile, Adendorf lies straight ahead, obscured by dense woodland to the left of the road. At the end of the trees, the road swings left into the village main street (3).

The first vehicles to pass along this road were armoured cars of the 89th Reconnaissance Squadron. They came under fire as they rounded the corner, but the sight of halftracks and tanks entering the village quickly brought an end to the German resistance. After sending the prisoners to the rear, Task Force Engeman was on the move once more.

Now follow the road through the **centre of Adendorf**, heading

Berkum to Remagen.

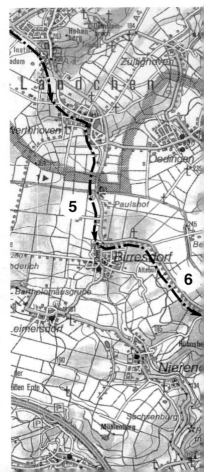

166

Lieutenant Timmermann's view of Arzdorf.

towards Arzdorf a mile away. The countryside once more becomes
open beyond the outskirts of the village and Fritzdorf, the southern
column's second objective, can be seen on the high ground in the
distance to the right of the road (4).

As the head of 27th Armored Infantry Battalion column
approached the outskirts of Arzdorf, they were targeted by anti-
tank weapons and small arms fire. This time the Germans had
deployed in the wooded area immediately north of the village.

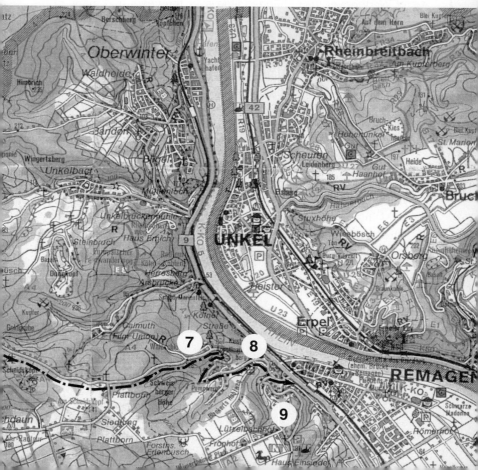

While A Company dismounted and fanned out into the fields either side of the road, the tanks and halftracks moved slowly into the village. The German rearguard soon surrendered and Timmermann's men rejoined their vehicles on the far side of the village.

Continue straight on through Arzdorf, following the main road as it swings first left, then right before heading straight up the slope. A ¹/₄ mile beyond the crest of the hill, turn right at the crossroads on the outskirts of Berkum, signposted for Werthhoven. As you head south, take note of the magnificent panorama to the left, the wooded hills of the Westerwald on the far side of the Rhine.

Colonel Engeman's reconnaissance vehicles encountered no resistance along this part of the route and the armoured column was able to move quickly across the open countryside.

After ¹/₂ mile take the **right turn into Werthhoven** and keep to the main road, Ahrtalstrasse, as you enter the village,. The centre of Werthhoven has changed little over the years and many of the houses that line the narrow street at the bottom of the hill look the same as they did in March 1945. Following the main road as it turns sharp right at the bottom of the slope, head through the modern outskirts. At the far end of Werthhoven **turn right at the crossroads**, signposted for Birresdorf. The road climbs a gentle slope and at the summit of the hill after ¹/₄ mile, look to park on the right, next to a small covered reservoir (5). If you walk fifty metres along the verge past the grassy mound, it is possible to view large parts of the route taken by the southern column.

52nd Armored Infantry Battalion advanced from right to left through a series of small villages. Fritzdorf is to the west, with its white church tower (electricity pylons stand just behind), next came Oeverich and Leimersdorf as the column headed east meeting no organised resistance. The column bypassed

Looking southwest across the southern column's route to Sinzig.

Fritzdorf

Oeverich

Scheidskopf

Birresdorf →

Task Force Engeman came under fire as it approached the woods overlooking Birresdorf.

Birresdorf, the village on the lower slopes of the hill immediately to the south. Most Germans had fled by this stage towards the Rhine and those cut off by the rapid American advance were sent to the rear as prisoners of war. The GIs were pleased to see white flags hanging from windows as they made their way towards its final objective, Sinzig. The town lies hidden in the Ahr valley to the south.

Return to your car and **continue south towards Birresdorf**, turning left for Remagen before it enters the outskirts, and head east for the wooded slopes of the Scheidskopf (6).

As Task Force Engeman approached the edge of the woods, the head of the column came under small arms fire from the tree line. Once again Timmermann's men dismounted while the heavy calibre guns on the halftracks and tanks opened fire. It was a one sided battle, and within minutes the infantry rearguard emerged with their hands up.

Follow the road through the dense woods noting how the ground drops away steeply at several points.

Major Cothran, Brigadier Hoge's intelligence officer, managed to catch up the column as it travelled thought the woods and passed on the information about the bridge to Colonel Engeman. Although the news instilled a sense of

The wooded slopes of the Scheidskopf were an ideal place for an ambush.

urgency into the advance, Engeman was reluctant to speed up because the thick woods were an ideal place for an ambush.

After passing the minor side road signposted for Bad Neuenhar and Ahrweiler (Plattborn junction), the road begins to descend down the eastern slops of the Scheidskopf. Half a mile beyond the

The Waldschlösschen Tavern

junction there is a small cluster of houses hidden in the trees to the left of the road; an imposing structure, known locally as Waldschlösschen, stands alongside the road just beyond (7).

The building was a tavern in March 1945 and as Lieutenant Timmermann cross-examined the owners, Lieutenant Burrows called to him from the woods to the right of the road. Although the area is now covered by thick woodland, sixty years ago the trees ended a short distance away. Timmermann joined Burrows on the tree line and the two stared in amazement at Rhine valley and the Ludendorff Bridge.

It is impossible to stand on the same spot and see the Rhine as the two officers; a dense plantation obscures the view. It is however, possible to view it from a similar position later on if you are prepared for a steep climb.

Beyond the Waldschlösschen the road begins to descend rapidly in a series of hairpin bends, as it snakes its way down into Remagen. There are plenty of warning signs relating to the road conditions ahead; take careful note of them. After Lieutenant Timmermann had reconnoitred the outskirts of Remagen, he led A Company down the steep slope to the left of the road on foot. Meanwhile, Captain Soumas and his four Pershing tanks led C Company in their halftracks down the road. Although there are brief glimpses of the valley below through the trees to the left of the road, drivers are advised to concentrate on their driving; there are plenty of opportunities to study the view safely in a short while.

The American view over the Rhine - *45 minutes*
As the road levels out there is a sign for the Apollinaris Church to the left; pull in to a small car park alongside the road to the left (8). Follow the driveway up to the church and pass through the gate to

The Apollinaris Church overlooks Remagen.

The view along the Rhine from the church terrace.

the right hand side of the church door to view a spectacular panorama of Rhine valley from the terrace. If the gates to the terrace are locked, follow the path down the hill below the church, following a series of statues representing the Stations of the Cross. It is possible to get a similar view from alongside Station VI as the path descends towards the town.

Having passed the church Timmermann's men made their way into the town, following the high street through the centre. Erpeler Ley, the huge basalt outcrop on the far bank, dominates the horizon and it is just possible to make out the twin bridge towers at the foot of the cliff.

It is possible to climb the steep hill behind the church to view the Rhine, however, the path is steep and in wet weather it can be quite slippery. Heading out of the church grounds turn right and after a 20 metres climb the steep flight of steps to the left. At the top of the steps the path winds through the woods to a shrine that stands on a small viewing terrace. It is possible to look back over the roof of the Apollinaris Church and across the Rhine valley.

Lieutenant Timmermannn's view of the bridge, 'Dammit, that's the Rhine; I didn't think it was that close.'

To reach the top of the hill, follow the path behind the shrine as it climbs through the woods. After 200 metres the path levels out; take the path to the left leading to a picnic shelter. Although Timmermann and Engeman stood several hundred metres to the right as they looked on the Ludendorff Bridge for the first time, the view from the shelter is similar.

Having studied the impressive panorama, retrace your steps back to the Apollinaris Church and your car. Note that the slopes were bare when A Company descended the slope to reach Remagen and they could see German troops withdrawing across the bridge in the distance.

The German view over the Rhine - *15 minutes*
Heading down the hill towards Remagen, take the right turning into Waldbergstrasse after 400m (signposted for Auf der Neide). Following the narrow road as it winds its way up the hill through modern housing. Turn sharp right at the summit in front of a small car park and park your car close to a small traffic island after 200 metres. Follow the overgrown tarmac track through the woods to the right and after 150 metres keep to the right as the track forks. In a few metres the track swings round to the left into what used to be the courtyard of the Waldberg Hotel (9).

Although the building was once a fine hotel with commanding views of the Rhine, it has fallen into a state of disrepair in recent years. The structure is in a dangerous condition and should not be entered. Follow the path to the right of the building through the bushes and after a few metres it is possible to look across what remains of the hotel gardens and the Rhine valley beyond.

Captain Bratge had sent Sergeant Rothe and the Bridge Security Company to the hotel on the evening of 6 March 1945 to keep a lookout for advancing American troops. While Rothe stationed outposts along the Victoriasberg heights he waited at the hotel for news. Although bushes obscure the view to the

The ruins of the Waldberg Hotel.

north and south it is easy to see why Bratge wanted his men stationed on the heights.

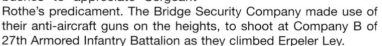

A little further on there is another gap in the bushes and it is possible to view the Rhine north of Remagen. The Apollinaris Church is a useful landmark on the hill north of the town and Sergeant Rothe could see A Company's men as they descended into the town and after failing to contact Captain Bratge by telephone, he realised his only option was to run down to the bridge to raise the alarm. Rothe was wounded several times as he made his escape and by the time he arrived at the towers Captain Bratge had withdrawn to the east bank.

As you make your way back, take a second look through the bushes to appreciate Sergeant Rothe's predicament. The Bridge Security Company made use of their anti-aircraft guns on the heights, to shoot at Company B of 27th Armored Infantry Battalion as they climbed Erpeler Ley.

Return to your car and retrace your route, turning right at the junction at the bottom of the hill. After 200 metres turn left onto Remagen bypass and then take the first right into the town, crossing over the railway. Park you car in one of the car parks in the centre of the town.

Walking tour of Remagen -1 *hour*
Remagen's railway station (*Bahnhof*) at the end of Bahnhofstrasse, in the centre of the town, is the starting point for the tour. Head west along Drususstrasse parallel to the railway, The street is named in honour of the Roman general who established the first settlement on the west bank of the Rhine. At the junction of Rümerplatz, on the right after 100 metres, a small memorial garden stands on the site of Remagen's synagogue (1). The building was destroyed by fire on Kristallnacht, in November 1938.

Continue 150 metres along Drususstrasse to an underpass

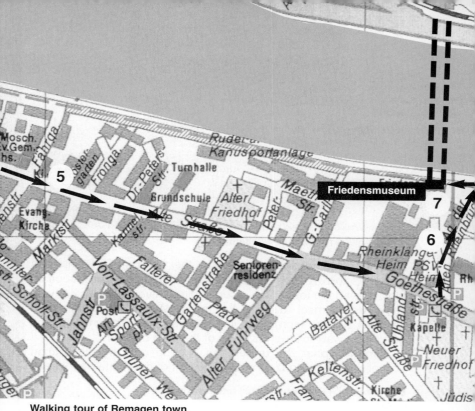

Walking tour of Remagen town.

beneath the railway (2). Timmermann's company approached the town down the slope in front, past the Apollinaris church. They entered the town via Bachstrasse, the narrow street to the right. Captain Soumas' Pershing tanks came down the road across the

Remagen's railway station.

Remembering Remagen's synagogue.

railway before turning right along the bypass. C Company's halftracks followed the tanks before splitting into three groups as they entered the town. One group (typically five halftracks carrying half a dozen men) followed the tanks, while the second group followed Timmermann's men into the heart of the town. The next part of the walk follows the route of the third column.

Continue past the underpass, turning right by the Roman Catholic Church into Deichweg. The start of the Rhine promenade

Bachstrasse, A Company's route into the town.

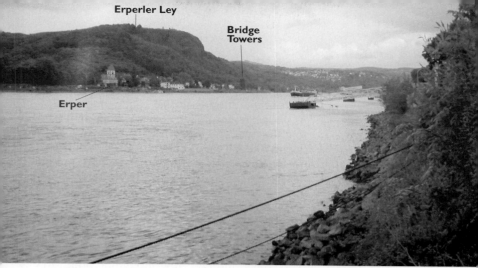

View along the promenade, the bridge towers stand at the foot of Erpeler Ley.

is at the bottom of the slope and as you turn right by the river it worth spending some time studying the impressive panorama (3).

While standing close to the river, it is easy to see why the German Armies were desperate to cross the Rhine ahead of the American spearheads. It was, and still is an impressive barrier; at over 300 metres its wide fast flowing waters presented Von Rundstedt with a natural barrier to regroup behind. Although it is difficult to spot the twin bridge towers that stand on the west bank of the river, it is possible to see the identical pair on the opposite bank at the foot Erpeler Ley.

Head along the promenade and after 150m turn right under an arch into Pintgasse. The market place is at the top of a short hill (4) and Remagen's tourist information office is on the immediate right as you enter the square. A Company entered the square along Bachstrasse to the immediate left of the town hall (Rathaus). Although the majority of German soldiers had fled by the time Timmermann's men entered the town, the GIs moved warily through the narrow streets while the local population looked on.

To follow A Company's route turn left into Marktstrasse heading along the pedestrian precinct. Although the shop fronts are modern, the upper storeys of many buildings have changed little since 1945. After 200m Bahnhofstrasse joins from the right and it is possible to see the railway station at the far end.

Remagen's Town Hall.

St Anne's convent.

Head straight on at the end of the pedestrian precinct; St Anne's Convent is on the left after 75m (5). *Hauptmann* Bratge used part of the building for his headquarters and it is possible that Major Scheller found him here on the morning of 7 March. Continue east along Altestrasse through the modern outskirts of the town. Remagen has expanded in post war years but in 1945 the area was quite open and A Company would have had a clear view of the bridge.

250m beyond the town cemetery follow the main road, Goethestrasse, as it forks to the left, signposted for Kripp and the Sports Centre. As you pass through the industrial area, the towers can be seen behind the warehouses on the left. Turn left into a side road after 200m, by the signpost for 'Brücke von Remagen'. A few metres from the junction a grass path heads up a slope to the left through an avenue of small trees. From the viewing platform at the top (6) it is possible to see the bridge towers from the same perspective as Timmermann's men did on the afternoon of 7 March. The GIs saw the explosion rock the bridge as they prepared to cross and the mixed emotions they must have felt when they saw that it was still standing are difficult to comprehend. Although the bridge is no longer there it is possible to visualise what a daunting prospect it must have been for A Company as they ran onto the bridge. Although the two towers directly in front were unoccupied, machine guns in the towers at the far end opened fire as soon as the men began to cross.

There are two ways of reaching the entrance to the museum (7) at the foot of the right hand tower. The first involves returning to the road and walking down to the river. The second route is shorter but involves climbing down the steep path, running alongside the viaduct wall.

Friedensmuseum Brücke von Remagen - *1 hour*

The towers stood unoccupied and forgotten until the 1960s when Hans Peter Kürten, Mayor of Remagen, decided to try and create a museum dedicated to peace. Attempts to raise government funding failed and for seven years Kürten tried in vain to purchase the land from the German Federal Railways. In 1976 engineers began to remove the bridge piers from the Rhine to make it safer for river traffic. Kürten decided to try and sell small pieces of the piers

The bridge towers now house a museum dedicated to world peace.

encased in synthetic resin to the public and launched the scheme on 7 March 1978, the 33rd anniversary of the crossing. The scheme was an unexpected success and over the next two years Kürten managed to raise over 100,000 DM. With the cooperation with the local employment office, local labour restored the towers to their former glory and on 7 March 1980 the project was realised when the first of over 500,000 visitors entered the museum.

Outside the museum take note of the memorial plaques on the base of the towers. A number of markers indicate how far the Rhine can rise when it is in flood. The entrance fee is 3.5 euros for adults and one euro for children; group discounts are available on request. In the first room, just beyond the admission booth, is a gallery of photographs depicting the bridge from its construction during the First World War to its collapse thirty years later. Climb the spiral staircase to the next exhibition, bypassing the corridor leading to the second tower. The photographs depict life in Remagen during the air raids throughout the winter of 1944-45; there is a memorial roll remembering those who lost their lives. The second floor contains photographs and memorabilia of the officers and men who manned the bridge; the American crossing is covered on the third floor. The top floor remembers the prisoner of war camp that occupied the area south of Remagen. Between April and June 1945

9th Armormed Division's memorial.

Elements of the 78th Division bore the brunt of the German counterattacks.

99th Division was the first complete division across the Rhine.

The memorial for Remagen's local Regiment.

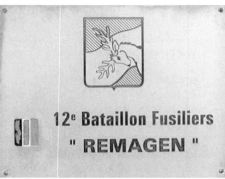

For thirty years the bridge piers posed a serious obstacle to river traffic. National Archives 111-SC-458076

over 300,000 German soldiers were held in temporary camps while the Allies restored order across post war Germany.

Retrace your steps down to the gallery that leads across to the second tower. The large ground floor room contains photographs and documents relating to the design and construction of the bridge between 1916 and 1918, while the floor above contains material covering the making of David Wolper's film *The Bridge at Remagen* in 1969. The remainder of the tower is devoted to the main theme of the museum, world peace. An exhibition contains a list of the wars that there have been since 1945 and is a bleak reminder that the world remains to be a violent place for many.

After visiting the museum make your way back along the promenade to the centre of the town.

Car Tour 2
The East Bank - *1½ hours*

After returning to your car head out of the town along the road towards the bridge towers, following signs for Kripp. Half a mile after passing the towers there is a crucifix and memorial to the left of the road, opposite Remagen college (1). Turn right into the side road and find a temporary parking space in the car park. Although the Americans remember Remagen for the capture of the Ludendorff Bridge, thousands of Germans remembered the town for entirely different reasons. As the war drew to a close the Allies were overwhelmed with thousands of prisoners of war and temporary camps were set up across Germany to hold them until resistance ended. Although they were initially designed to hold 50,000 men, the enclosure at Remagen eventually housed 134,000 men and women, another at Sinzig held 118,500.

Conditions along the 'Golden Mile', as the area is known locally, were primitive and resources were limited as the Allies struggled to cope with the influx of prisoners. Many were forced to sleep in the open air or in makeshift shelters and poor diet encouraged disease to spread. 62nd US Field Hospital, assisted by German doctors and medics, struggled to cope and over the course of three months more than five hundred prisoners died from ill health. They were buried together near Bodendorf along with other POWs who died in the temporary camps.

In the 1980s Hans Kürten discovered a statue of the Madonna in the vicarage at Kripp. A prisoner at one of the camps, Professor Adolf Wamper, had made the statue out of mud. Kürten preserved the

An aerial view of the 'Golden Mille' prisoner of war camp. National Archives 111-SC-205235

The shrine erected to remember the prisoners of war held in the Golden Mile camps.

The preserved black Madonna statue.

statue in oil and set about raising funds for a memorial dedicated to the prisoners. The chapel was dedicated in October 1987 as a permanent reminder of the camps.

Continue south into Kripp and at the T-junction in the centre of the village turn left. Follow the road round to the left at the bottom of the hill and the ferry is a short distance in front. The Linz Ferry (2) operates a regular service, running constantly between the two banks of the Rhine. Cyclists are charged one euro; cars cost two euros. On the far side, follow the side road to the right as it runs parallel to the main highway; it swings round to meet it at a T-junction after 200 metres, turn left for Honnef and Bonn heading north. The road bypasses Linz and travels on the east bank of the river. Before long Remagen comes into view on the far bank and the bridge towers can be seen ahead on the right hand side of the road; park in the layby opposite the towers (3).

Sergeant DeLisio entered the right hand tower, capturing a lone German, while Sergeant Chinchar took two men into the left hand tower. While his comrades were busy clearing the

182

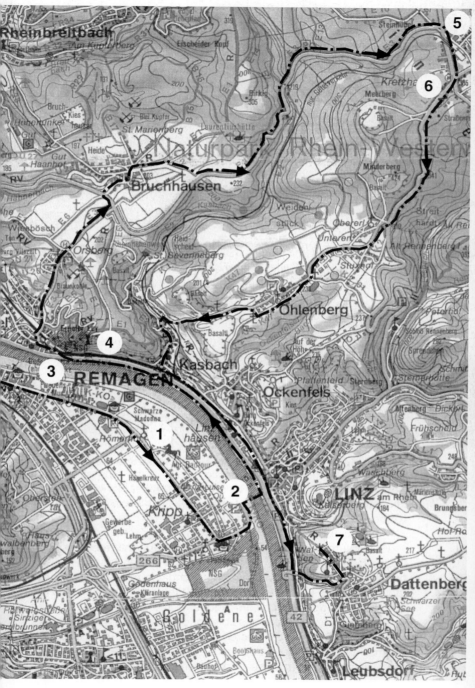

Car tour of the east bank of the Rhine.

The pontoon bridge connecting Kripp and Linz. National Archives 111-SC-331839

A similar view of the Linz ferry, the Kaiserberg looks over the town.

towers Sergeant Drabik carried on covering the last few yards to become the first US soldier to set foot on the east bank of the Rhine.

Walk south alongside the road and after 200 metres cross over, taking care of the busy traffic, and pass under a small railway bridge. Heading left follow the track alongside the railway line; the tunnel entrance is to the right after 200 metres. The tunnel mouth was bricked up many years ago and the tunnel now houses seismic instruments. It is possible to look over the wall to the left and see the German view across the river beyond the towers. As Timmermann's men gathered on the far bank, Captain Friesenhahn tried in vain to destroy the bridge, sending men out to blow the

The bridge towers on the east bank.

back up charges when the primary circuits failed. Once A Company had crossed it set up roadblocks on the main road about 200 metres north and south of the bridge. The GIs then had to wait all evening before tanks were able cross the bridge. Retrace your steps back to your car.

Heading north, take the side road to the right after 200 metres, signposted for Orsberg. Follow the road through Erpel, making a sharp right across the railway. The road crosses a second railway bridge (the disused railway that once passed through the tunnel

The sealed up entrance to the rail tunnel.

and across the bridge), after 100 metres; Major Scheller made his escape along the cutting that runs beneath the road. The tunnel mouth lies hidden in the trees to the right.

Turn right just beyond the bridge, signposted for Erpeler Ley and head up the steep winding road as it climbs to the summit of the basalt outcrop. B Company of 27th Armored Infantry Battalion scaled the slopes to occupy the hill, suffering heavy casualties from AA guns in the valley below. There is a restaurant and bar at the top of the hill, park you car in the spaces nearby (4).

Follow the path to the cross on the edge of the cliff to take in the

spectacular views across Remagen and the Rhine. It is possible to follow the events on 7 March 1945 from the viewpoint, tracing Lieutenant Timmermann's route through the town to the bridge. The views to the south across Kasbach, Ohlenberg, Linz and Dattenberg are equally impressive.

Return to your car and retrace your route back into Erpel and head straight on at the T-junction by the railway bridge, head up the hill out of the village to Orsberg. 27th Armored Infantry Battalion captured the village on the night of 7 March, stopping German engineers reaching the bridge. Continue through Orsberg and turn left at the T-junction after a mile. Take the first right after 200 metres and follow the main street through Bruchhausen, which was cleared on the afternoon of 8 March by the 2/47th Infantry Regiment. The road passes through open fields on the far side of Bruchhausen and the wooded hills of the Westerwald dominate the

The memorial on the summit of Erpeler Ley

The view over the suburbs of Remagen, the Ahr valley is in the distance.

Bridge Towers

Golden Mile

The view south towards Linz.

horizon. It is easy to see how the German managed to thwart attempts to push east of Bruchhausen.

Half a mile beyond the village turn left at the T-junction heading for Kretzhaus. The road enters thick woods and as it winds its way along the side of a steep gorge. Take care driving along this road, as it negotiates a number of hairpin bends (switch on your headlights if necessary).

Infantry were forced to pick their way along the sides of deep ravines, constantly harried by snipers and mortars, while tanks made easy targets for hidden anti-tank guns as they edged forward along the narrow roads. There are occasional glimpses of the valley to the right through the trees, which 310th Infantry Regiment advanced along as it tried to scale the twin peaks of Meerberg and Minderberg overlooking Kretzhaus.

The road climbs through the woods and after two miles turn right at the T-junction, known as 'Hell's Corner'. (5) As 52nd Armored Infantry Battalion advanced through the woods towards the junction tanks, 88mm anti-tank guns and infantry confronted them. Lieutenant McCurdy led his platoon up to the junction, directing tank destroyers forward to knock them out.

Tanks were confined to the narrow roads, while infantry had to scale steep wooded ravines.

Head under the railway bridge into Kretzhaus, where 310th

187

Hell's
Corner

Looking north from the crossroads towards Hell's Corner.

Infantry Regiment fought for five days to gain control of the vital
crossroads. Time after time the infantry were driven back by artillery
and mortar fire as they tried to engage infantry dug in around the
village. The American Shermans and Tank Destroyers were driven
back several times by a Tiger tank sat on the crossroads; meanwhile,
Panzer IVs and Self Propelled guns patrolled the hamlet.

At the staggered crossroads (6), keep to the main road as it
swings to the right, (there is a service station at the crossroads. It
one of the few in the area and a useful stop off point if you need
any provisions for the rest of your journey) and follow the
Ohlenberg road as it descends through the woods. Tanks, trying to
support 310th Infantry Regiment's attack on the crossroads
encountered hidden anti-tank positions as they tried to advance up
the road. 47th Infantry Regiment advanced up the valley to the left

Bitter fighting raged for five days around Kretzhaus crossroads.

of the road, capturing the twin peaks of Rennenberg I and II before closing in on the village of Notscheid.

One mile from Kretzhaus, turn right into the side road signposted for Ohlenberg as the road emerges from the woods. After passing through the hamlet of Orbrunt it is possible to see the Rhine valley below. Half a mile further on the road turns sharp right into Ohlenberg; follow the one-way system through the village.

During the early days of the bridgehead, the Germans made several counterattacks into Ohlenberg in the hope of reaching the river. On the morning of 10 March German armour managed to break through 3/47th Infantry Regiment's positions, as they drove into the village the tanks and halftracks encountered 2/310th Infantry Regiment, which had just arrived. Rather than finding themselves in a reserve position, the men had to fight where they stood, driving the Germans from the village.

At the far end of the Ohlenberg turn sharp right and continue down the hillside into Kasbach. Turn left onto the main road heading back along the riverbank towards Linz and half a mile after the ferry; take the slip road to the right, signposted for Dattenberg. The side road doubles back over the main highway before climbing up the steep hill towards the village. Just beyond the village nameplate, turn sharp left at a hairpin bend. This section of road is quite narrow and you have to be prepared to let others pass before you drive into the village. Carry straight on at the crossroads and after 200 metres turn left into a housing estate, heading down the slope to a small parking area at the end of the estate (7). It is possible to see Remagen and Erpeler Ley from the vantage point and it is worth walking a short distance along the tracks fanning out from the parking area to take full advantage of the views.

After taking one last look at the Rhine, retrace your steps through the housing estate and as you approach the sharp left turn leading out of the estate, take note of the 'chateau' on the horizon. The 1st Battalion of 310th Infantry Regiment fought a fierce battle around the building, a German headquarters.

Head back through Dattenberg and make your way back to the Linz ferry. Alternatively head north for Bonn or south for Koblenz, following Autobahn 42 along the east bank of the Rhine.

German troops advanced down the Ohlenberg road several times to try and reach the bridge.

Ohlenberg

INDEX